NO MAN'S LAND

Doug Tatum is the Founding Partner and Chairman Emeritus of Tatum, LLC, the nation's largest and fastest-growing financial and technology executive services and consulting firm, with over one thousand professionals and thirty-three offices across the country. He currently serves as the Chairman and CEO of The Co-investment Partnership, a private equity co-investment fund organized for the benefit of Tatum's partners and employees, and serves on the board of Seraph Group, a unique venture capital firm specializing in providing capital to emerging growth companies. He is a recognized expert on the capital markets and entrepreneurial growth businesses and has testified before Congress on more than one occasion concerning United States tax policy and the financing issues faced by growing companies. Tatum's insights into the No Man's Land transition facing growing companies have been published in a number of magazines and journals. He is a highly sought after speaker for business groups both in the United States and internationally. He lives on a farm outside Atlanta.

NO MAN'S LAND

- A Survival Manual for Growing Midsize Companies

DOUG TATUM

PORTFOLIO

PORTFOLIO
Published by the Penguin Group
Penguin Group (USA) Inc., 375 Hudson Street, New York, New York 10014, U.S.A. •
Penguin Group (Canada), 90 Eglinton Avenue East, Suite 700, Toronto, Ontario, Canada
M4P 2Y3 (a division of Pearson Penguin Canada Inc.) • Penguin Books Ltd, 80 Strand,
London WC2R 0RL, England • Penguin Ireland, 25 St Stephen's Green, Dublin 2, Ire-
land (a division of Penguin Books Ltd) • Penguin Group (Australia), 250 Camberwell
Road, Camberwell, Victoria 3124, Australia (a division of Pearson Australia Group Pty Ltd)
• Penguin Books India Pvt Ltd, 11 Community Centre, Panchsheel Park, New Delhi – 110
017, India • Penguin Group (NZ), 67 Apollo Drive, Rosedale, North Shore 0632, New
Zealand (a division of Pearson New Zealand Ltd) • Penguin Books (South Africa) (Pty)
Ltd, 24 Sturdee Avenue, Rosebank, Johannesburg 2196, South Africa

Penguin Books Ltd, Registered Offices: 80 Strand, London WC2R 0RL, England

First published in the United States of America by Portfolio,
a member of Penguin Group (USA) Inc. 2007
This paperback edition with a new preface published 2008

Copyright © Tatum LLC, 2007, 2008
All rights reserved

Drawings by Samuel Sharpe. Graphs and digital illustrations by Chip Evans.

THE LIBRARY OF CONGRESS HAS CATALOGED THE HARDCOVER EDITION AS FOLLOWS:
Tatum, Doug.
No man's land : what to do when your company is too big to be small but too small
to be big / Doug Tatum.
  p. cm.
Includes bibliographical references and index.
ISBN 978-1-59184-172-2 (hc.)
ISBN 978-1-59184-249-1 (pbk.)
1. Small business—Management. 2. Small business. I. Title.
HD62.7.T38 2007
658.4'06—dc22   2007009388

Printed in the United States of America
Set in Janson Text
Designed by Katy Riegel

Except in the United States of America, this book is sold subject to the condition that it shall
not, by way of trade or otherwise, be lent, resold, hired out, or otherwise circulated without
the publisher's prior consent in any form of binding or cover other than that in which it is
published and without a similar condition including this condition being imposed on the subsequent purchaser.

The scanning, uploading and distribution of this book via the Internet or via any other means
without the permission of the publisher is illegal and punishable by law. Please purchase only
authorized electronic editions, and do not participate in or encourage electronic piracy of
copyrighted materials. Your support of the author's rights is appreciated.

To my wife, Lynda, whose life is living proof
of the truth of the ancient proverb:

Her husband is known in the gates,
when he sits among the elders of the land.

———————

— PROVERBS 31:23

Acknowledgments

My brother, John Tatum, talked me into working with him to build what today is a national firm that bears our name. I can still vividly remember writing No Man's Land and the four Ms with him on a paper napkin in a Mexican restaurant off Chamblee Tucker Road in Atlanta. John and I were engaged in an intellectual discussion about the patterns we saw in our clients' businesses—something we have done so many times over the years. John was truly my first editor and collaborator. His intense focus on the purity of a simple idea prompted me to spend a decade examining the concepts in this book. Without his encouragement and contributions, this book never would have seen the light of day.

I also want to thank the men and women who shared their stories with me. You are my heroes. You had the courage to share with every entrepreneurial leader who reads this book the ups, downs, doubts, and victories of leading a company into, out of, and, in some cases, back into and through No Man's Land. This book is your story and I hope you believe I have done your experiences justice.

To my partners in the firm, who I trust will preserve the traditions and values that have made our firm a success: Thank you so much for allowing me the time and resources necessary to complete this book. Many of you in the firm have not only encouraged me to get this book written but have taken the time to expose this material to thousands of companies over the years. Your feedback has reinforced my belief that the concepts shared in the book are universal to the experiences of entrepreneurs. I would not have lifted a pen to start without my partners' confirmation.

I'd also like to thank Seth "the assassin" Schulman, whose collaboration from beginning to end made this work possible. Seth, you are now a lifelong friend, a partner in crime on this book, and one of the most incredible and talented people I have ever had the opportunity to work with.

To Jane Pass, thank you so much for your dedication in helping me pull this off. I couldn't have done it without you.

And finally to Mom, you gave me the love of reading and the appreciation for a good story well told.

Preface

Since the original publication of *No Man's Land*, I have been privileged to speak before thousands of entrepreneurs about the material in this book. It never ceases to amaze me how the concept of the No-Man's-Land transition and the 4 M navigational rules—the seemingly simplest of concepts—can have such an enormous impact on the lives of entrepreneurial business leaders. As always, the most interesting part of the journey for me has been the opportunity to meet and hear the stories of the amazing men and women who have the courage and stamina to start and grow a business in today's chaotic world. In fact, I am even more convinced after talking with policy makers, political pundits, and economists interested in the premise of *No Man's Land* that the talents of the American entrepreneur are more important than ever before. For instance:

- The economy needs companies that can grow out of the small business category. It's these emerging growth companies that add new jobs and help the economy grow.
- Large companies need growing entrepreneurial companies and the private equity investors that invest in them because

it's these emerging companies that innovate within their markets. America's large corporations depend on a constant supply of new companies to acquire in order to refresh their product lines and keep them competitive on the world markets. Entrepreneurial growth companies that break out of the pack and grow have become corporate America's de facto R&D.

- Innovation born and bred in the United States by entrepreneurial growth companies can stay in the United States—even if the manufacturing and servicing of it moves abroad.

Just before the publication of this paperback edition of *No Man's Land,* I participated in an economic forum held in China put together by Chinese government officials to encourage the development of Chinese emerging growth companies and the private equity firms that invest in them. There were several thousand people in attendance. That conference should serve as a stark reminder of just how important it is for our government to think carefully about anything that makes it more difficult for U.S. entrepreneurs to start, grow, and capitalize their businesses.

This book is all about a tough but rewarding journey for America's best ideas developed by America's most important economic competitive assets—its entrepreneurs and the businesses that they lead through adolescence.

Godspeed on the journey.

Contents

Introduction

If you're an entrepreneur leading a rapidly growing firm, or if you aspire to lead a rapid-growth firm someday, then hang on, you're in for a rough ride. Nine out of ten start-ups in this country fail within the first three years.[1] Fast-growth companies—or gazelles, as former MIT professor David Birch has called them*—are on the verge of breaking out, yet a sizable percentage of these fail as well. Of those that don't fail, most can't sustain their rapid growth rate for very long. Research has shown that of firms that make it onto *Inc.* magazine's Inc. 500 list of rapidly growing companies each year, only one in three manage to return the following year.[2]

In his book *Blueprint to a Billion,* David G. Thomson tracks growth patterns for a portfolio of firms that reached $1 billion in revenue after going public. As Thomson demonstrates, only a select number of companies (approximately 5 percent of the 7,454 that

---

*Dr. Birch has single-handedly pioneered the academic study of rapid-growth firms. In coining the widely used term "gazelles," he has argued that the economy's business sector is divided among three distinct types of firms: "mice" (i.e., small companies), "elephants" (large, established companies), and "gazelles." Birch defines gazelles as companies with an average revenue growth rate of at least 20 percent over a four-year period.

went public since 1980) reached escape velocity and continued to grow to $1 billion. Those that did experienced exponential growth only after transitioning through an inflection point that occurred in some cases as early as $10 million in revenue, but that took place, on average, at $50 million.[3]

As the graph below shows, thousands of public and private firms each year approach a similar juncture in their development, an inflection point at which they are transformed from small to large, from upstarts to new business categories, from intriguing ideas to America's de facto research and development department. What the graph also shows, however, is that the vast majority of growing public and private companies reach this inflection point only to crash and burn. Likewise, a far smaller but still significant number of firms reach this inflection point and make a conscious decision to stay small.

We worship successful entrepreneurs such as Bill Gates and Steve Jobs and avidly seek their secrets to success. As Bo Burlingham has written, "The notion that bigger—and more—is better has so pervaded our culture that most people assume all entrepreneurs want to capitalize on every business opportunity, grow their companies as fast as they can, and build the next Microsoft or Citicorp."[4] Yet growth isn't necessarily all it's cracked up to be. And even when growing companies do flourish, the conditions of success are often not what their owners bargained for. Growing a company to scale confronts the leadership team with unforeseen challenges that can strain them to the point where they become embittered and wish their companies had remained small.

No Man's Land explores the reality of growth by focusing on a pivotal stage in a business's life cycle, the adolescent stage in which a rapidly growing firm is too big to be small, but too small to be big. This stage is precisely the inflection point documented by both Thomson and Birch in their respective bodies of research. During this phase—I call it No Man's Land—growth confronts entrepre-

The *No Man's Land* Inflection Point

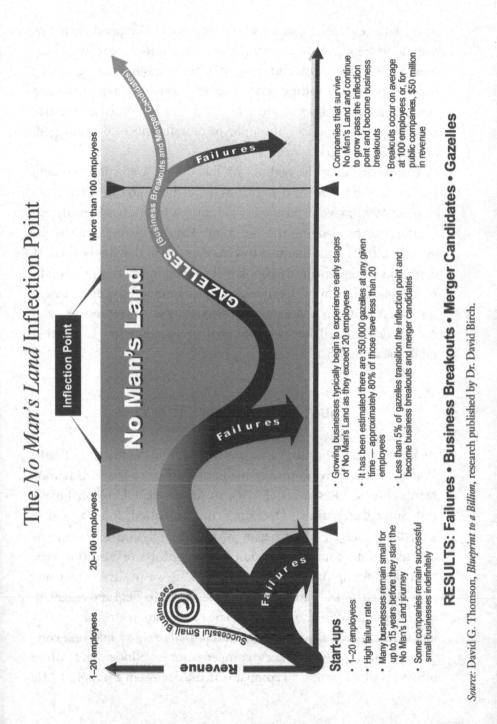

RESULTS: Failures • Business Breakouts • Merger Candidates • Gazelles

Start-ups
- 1–20 employees
- High failure rate
- Many businesses remain small for up to 15 years before they start the No Man's Land journey
- Some companies remain successful small businesses indefinitely

- Growing businesses typically begin to experience early stages of No Man's Land as they exceed 20 employees
- It has been estimated there are 350,000 gazelles at any given time — approximately 80% of those have less than 20 employees
- Less than 5% of gazelles transition the inflection point and become business breakouts and merger candidates

- Companies that survive No Man's Land and continue to grow pass the inflection point and become business breakouts
- Breakouts occur on average at 100 employees or, for public companies, $50 million in revenue

Source: David G. Thomson, *Blueprint to a Billion,* research published by Dr. David Birch.

neurs with new challenges for which they are ill-equipped. As in human adolescence, such growth should spark self-discovery and acquired discipline. Unfortunately, it often becomes an agonizing battle between the natural tendencies of a lonely entrepreneur and certain immutable laws of growth. The result is confusion, frustration, stagnation, and loss of employee morale, which, if prolonged, can lead to financial failure.

Comprehending the realities of this unique transition can help you make solid, informed decisions about how, and in some cases *whether*, to grow your business. And once a business is already expanding, acknowledging the No Man's Land transition and its inevitable pitfalls is the first step toward the success that lies beyond. If you're an entrepreneur, this book will put you in a better position to make your company all it can be, and, just as important, all you *want* it to be. And if you're dreaming of becoming an entrepreneur, then *No Man's Land* will provide essential preparation for a ride that might be wilder than you ever imagined.

JUST HOW WILD DOES IT GET?

As Burt Prater's story suggests, pretty wild. During the early 1990s, Prater left his thriving private medical practice to found Environmental Medical Resources (EMR), an Atlanta-based, national medical surveillance firm. Operating on borrowed money and a shoestring budget, EMR began to provide physical examinations and government-mandated medical reports for workers who were then cleaning up America's worst hazardous waste sites. The company thrived, quickly emerging as the leader in its field and receiving several rounds of investment from one of the nation's top private equity firms. Within six years, EMR was poised to sign a five-year contract to handle the worker's compensation, wellness, and safety programs of a Fortune 50 company. If the deal went through, EMR would double its annual revenues and gain a foothold in another new and potentially lucrative field, health and safety outsourcing. But signing the contract would require that EMR take on even more capital from its investors.

As the closing date drew near, Prater learned he would need to cede majority ownership of the company in order to obtain the necessary funds. He was shocked. Like many entrepreneurs, he had started a company so that he could experience the joys of working for himself. If he ceded majority ownership now, he would find himself working for someone else again—in this case, the capital markets. In addition, his employees—many of whom were close friends—would be left vulnerable to decisions made by third parties.

Given the financial stake required to handle the new contract, the

new endeavor's success would dictate whether Prater and his employees would actually wind up better off financially than they were before. Having started the company and seen it grow, did Prater really want to bet the firm on this new venture? Was this the deal of his life, or a deal with the devil?

Transitioning from Small to Big

Prater's decision was all the more difficult given recent changes in EMR's industry. During the 1980s, the government had set aside billions to clean up contaminated Superfund sites. To protect worker safety, federal law mandated that environmental contractors regularly screen their employees for industrial contaminants. EMR was the first company to offer this service on a national level. Developing a standardized protocol, EMR partnered with local clinics across the country to perform medical examinations, then it collected the data and created medical reports for the environmental contractors, thus greatly facilitating compliance with the law.

By the mid-1990s, however, stiff competition emerged, putting pressure on EMR's margins. In fact, just as Prater was struggling to evaluate his deal with the Fortune 50 company, he learned that he had lost his top customer, representing 20 percent of sales, to an aggressive underbidder. Talk about a dilemma: With EMR's core business becoming commoditized, could Prater really afford to pass on a deal that offered guaranteed revenue, as well as a chance to enter a new industry?

Prater remembers the period spent mulling over his big deal as one of the scariest in his life. "You have to understand," he says. "By the time I found out that I'd be ceding control of the company, we had already invested a million dollars preparing for this deal. The other side had announced it publicly. If I pulled out, I'd be disappointing a whole heck of a lot of people, including myself. Yet, I couldn't help but wonder if it was the right thing to do. Actually,

I didn't know what to do. For a while, I was miserable—a captain without a rudder."

. . .

So what happened to Prater? I'm afraid you'll have to read the book to find out. For now, I'll point out that the high failure rate of gazelles doesn't just hurt entrepreneurs and employees; it hurts everybody. Although gazelles are relatively few in number (no more than 5 percent of all American businesses),[5] they have a surprising and disproportionate impact on the economy, stimulating job creation and promoting research and product development.

As *Inc.* magazine has reported, emerging growth businesses created "practically as many jobs (10.7 million) as the entire U.S. economy (11.1 million)" from 1995 to 1999.[6] According to the National Commission on Entrepreneurship, growth firms create "two-thirds of all the new jobs; more than two-thirds of the innovation in the economy; and . . . two-thirds of the differences in economic growth rates among industrialized nations."[7] Conversely, when growth firms fail, American business cannot compete globally as well as it might. Our economy grows more slowly, and there are fewer new jobs.

Unlike other small businesses, gazelles—or rapidly growing firms—shake up markets, exerting pressure on larger public companies to innovate by introducing radically new solutions to existing customer problems. A select number of gazelles grow at breathtaking speed, transforming or creating entire business categories. As one academic report has explained, "not all businesses are dynamic and entrepreneurial. In fact, only five to ten percent of businesses in an economy are entrepreneurial ventures—introducing new ideas/methods/solutions to the production of goods and services in a market economy."[8] When acquired by larger firms, these businesses come to serve as corporate America's de facto research and development arm, giving us an edge over foreign competition.

I can't help but wonder: How many heart-wrenching disasters

would be prevented each year if entrepreneurs only understood from the outset how to manage around the inevitable pitfalls of No Man's Land? I wonder, too, how much less grief entrepreneurs would experience if only they realized that there were viable, satisfying alternatives to growth,[9] or if they knew that in choosing to grow at any cost they were embarking on a journey whose considerable pitfalls were not of their own making.

THE STORY OF NO MAN'S LAND

Everybody hates to field criticism about his or her professional decisions, but entrepreneurs truly detest it. Why? Because they *live* their businesses, investing not merely money but their hearts and souls. When their companies fail, it's a personal failure. And when someone questions the handling of their business, quite often it's taken as a personal affront.

Having worked as a senior executive officer at a number of national companies, as an adjunct professor of accounting, and as founding chairman and CEO of the national professional services firm that bears my name, I have watched emerging growth companies of various sizes and in various industries stumble and fall over the same fundamental issues. Some have been physically or financially unable to follow important changes in their customers' needs. Others had not developed a viable infrastructure for servicing increased demand, had not known how large they would need to become in order to pay for that infrastructure, or had failed to address the weaknesses of close friends and confidants who had made up their company's management team.

No matter how good their core business concepts, the companies I've seen have been pushed by growth into an uncomfortable situation where the resources and approaches that had allowed the firm to grow in the first place suddenly became insufficient and even an obstacle to further growth. Customers went away dissatisfied, and the entrepreneur in question felt disoriented, as if he or she were gradually and inexplicably losing control.

Entrepreneurial growth company CEOs and their supporting teams usually find it liberating to understand the transition they are facing in the context of broader patterns of business evolution. Once they realize that their firm's difficulties—stagnating sales, unhappy employees, inability to obtain credit, to name but a few—derive not from their own entrepreneurial instincts but from objective causes, they become much more willing to discuss the tough decisions they face as their companies drag them into uncharted territory.

"No Man's Land" captures the phenomenon of growing pains and brings it to life in a way that is meaningful to entrepreneurial leaders. The phrase is perfect, for it portrays this transitional stage in the life of a business as treacherous geographical terrain, which is how many entrepreneurs I know have actually experienced it.

Today I travel the country speaking about No Man's Land to groups of entrepreneurs and business leaders. Wherever I go, I get the same response. Listeners approach me with sadness in their eyes and say, "Doug, if only I had known about No Man's Land when I was running my company, we might still be in business." Others are more exuberant, describing their initial exposure to the idea of No Man's Land as an intense, almost cathartic experience. "You have to understand," they say. "It's so lonely growing a company. Nobody tells you what to do or how hard it's going to be. It's such a relief to know that I am not alone, that I am not to blame, and, most of all, that something can be done." The more I talk to entrepreneurs, the more convinced I become that No Man's Land is a widespread and potentially deadly phenomenon. The more, too, I want to help.

PROTECTING A NATIONAL TREASURE

The difficulties of the entrepreneurs I meet are haunting when you consider the broader context. We aren't doing nearly enough to nurture emerging growth companies—the backbone of our economy. On the contrary, so much of what we do today actually *impedes* gazelles' prospects. For instance, efforts to root out corporate corruption have resulted in new restrictions on the use of stock options as incentives—an important and even essential means of luring experienced executives to emerging growth companies. In addition, market forces have created a serious scarcity of capital in this country for mid-sized companies that need between $250,000 and $1 million— a group that includes many gazelles. Finally, regulatory changes related to Sarbanes-Oxley have dramatically changed the IPO market and increased the cost of capital for smaller public companies.

I have briefed policy makers in Congress, the SEC, and the Fed on a number of these and related issues. The more I speak with emerging growth company leaders, however, the more I realize that the greatest service that could be done for gazelles is simply to increase their and policy makers' awareness of No Man's Land as a transition that must be navigated for companies to grow to scale.

The entrepreneurs I encounter are routinely stymied by their inability to "get out of the weeds," to rise above chaotic operational firefighting and see their businesses in a new strategic light. To traverse No Man's Land, however, entrepreneurs need to become radically objective about their situation and knowledgeable about the strategic choices available to them.

They also need a plan.

THE FOUR *Ms*:
MARKET, MANAGEMENT, MODEL, AND MONEY

In analyzing the No Man's Land phenomenon, I have observed that the difficulties experienced by growing companies tend to fall into four distinct managerial areas. From this pattern, I've derived a series of fundamental navigational principles for managing a rapidly growing company:

- Understand the transition that will occur in the business's **Market**.
- Address the changes that will be required in its **Management**.
- Test its economic **Model** to assure continued profitability as the business scales upward.
- Understand the practical requirements for attracting the needed **Money**.

These four *Ms*—as I refer to them in this book—aren't merely theoretical constructs, but the fruit of prolonged marketplace observation. Consider, for example, the Market *M*. As businesses grow, they attract their first customers or clients on the strength of the entrepreneur's unique talents. Early customers gain the value of the entrepreneur's personal attention and efforts, receiving them in a relatively simple exchange. At a certain size, however, the physical demands become so intense that the entrepreneur can no longer deliver on an individual basis the value he or she once did. In particular, entrepreneurs can't keep up with evolving customer needs, or with the differing needs of new customers. As a result, misalignment arises, and the company experiences a number of breakdowns, including sales stagnation, quality problems, ineffective new product development, and customer service failures.

To manage the inevitable transformation of a company's market, an entrepreneur needs to realign his or her firm with its changing customer base so that product offerings remain relevant, the firm continues to deliver its core value proposition, and the firm remains simple to do business with. In other words, entrepreneurs need to ensure that their companies become good at what they themselves were initially good at. Only in this way will their firms continue to grow.

For entrepreneurs in the trenches, the four *Ms* are like Newton's observations about gravity—immutable laws for traversing No Man's Land. Difficult as it is, you as a business leader must step away from day-to-day operations and honestly evaluate yourself and your

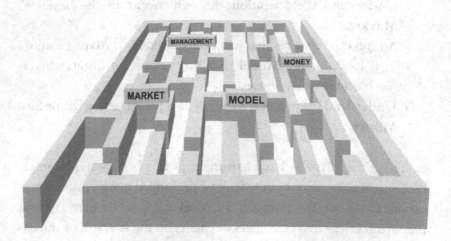

company in light of each of the four *M*s; otherwise, you will fail. I've seen it happen again and again.

The four *M*s are the intellectual foundation for our own firm's consulting CFO practice. We have applied the framework to hundreds of companies in all industries, helping entrepreneurial leaders anticipate and manage the difficulties inherent in growth. Our firm, Tatum, LLC, has flourished, becoming the nation's premier financial and technology leadership firm, with more than one thousand professionals in thirty-three cities.

More than just another how-to manual, *No Man's Land* is a cultural treatise that delves into the actual experience of running a rapidly growing company. In chapter 1, entrepreneurs tell what it's like to lead a fast-growth business and live through No Man's Land. Subsequent chapters analyze their stories, describing the hidden traps that confront and all too often sink even the most promising of firms as they expand. The navigational rules for passing safely through this treacherous terrain are elaborated on, and a series of tools designed to help the entrepreneur determine if his or her business is in No Man's Land is offered. At "pause points" located at the end of several chapters, you'll be encouraged to reflect strategically on the navigational rules and consider whether in fact you should grow. As you'll see, there are three possible endgames, aside from going out of business, from which all entrepreneurs in No Man's Land must choose: growing into a significant, category-defining firm; staying small; or selling out to a larger firm. At each of the successive pause points, you'll have a chance to mull over the various endgames from a steadily deepening perspective, an exercise that will equip you to determine which is the right path for you.

In chapter 7, the decision of whether or not to grow is approached more holistically, as you learn of the painful process Burt Prater went through in resolving his own dilemma. Chapter 8 closes the book by exploring the important contributions emerging growth firms make to the broader economy and suggesting how government might better help these firms to secure our nation's prosperity.

My ultimate objective in writing *No Man's Land* is to help lower the failure rate of this country's emerging growth businesses. I want to prevent entrepreneurs who have nurtured a wonderful idea from growing their firms right out of business. I want to help those first-, second-, or third-generation family members to understand what they are up against and what they need to consider in order to pass their businesses on to the next generation. I want to help those of you in the corporate world decide whether or not to jump ship and help grow a young company that you believe is onto something big.

If I can convince you that No Man's Land is a real transition, and that the navigational rules must be executed to keep the business growing, I will have succeeded in changing the way you react to day-to-day business problems. Many readers, I'm sure, will come away deeply disturbed in their notions about the journey ahead and the nature of the entrepreneurial challenge. But if I've done my job right, they'll also possess a much richer understanding of the microeconomics of business growth as well as the concrete tools they'll need if they are to succeed. They'll possess, in short, the basis for a new, more enduring hope.

1

Too Big to Be Small,
Too Small to Be Big

The entrepreneurs I know dream of rapid growth. Nothing exhilarates them so much as the thought of seeing the marketplace affirm a vision they had of doing something better or differently. Yet growing a successful business to scale is emotionally charged and risky. Time and again, I've seen firms catch fire only to grow themselves out of business. I've seen founders become exhausted and bitter from the strain of dealing with challenges that prove a lot more difficult and complex than they bargained for.

Rick Shelley understands the challenges of growth as well as anybody. In 1988, he founded First Standard Freight, Inc., a New York, New York–based firm that served as a customs broker and freight forwarder for companies shipping goods by land, sea, or air.[10] By the mid-1990s, business was taking off; First Standard was adding field offices and enjoying profit margins above the industry average. As Shelley explains, such success was especially sweet given where he had started. "My first office was a screened-in porch, my first desk, a door and cinder blocks. I didn't have a strategy, nor was I really good at the analytics of the business. I operated by flying by the seat of my pants, haphazardly. And there I was in 1995, 1996—really making it. What a feeling."

Unfortunately, the feeling did not last. By the late 1990s, Shelley's business was still growing, yet it was becoming more difficult for him to make money. To deliver on promises made to clients, First Standard had to invest in IT, accounting, and other back-office infrastructure in each of its branch offices. "All of a sudden, it seemed, we got into this heavy-duty profit-sucking mode of building overhead," Shelley says. "We were profitable, but eating capital at a huge rate. We were putting tons of money into the IT stuff—Web sites, visibility, value adds for our customers who wanted to track their containers. That was and still is the ugly part of our business."

To make matters worse, 9/11 came along, bringing with it a whole new set of government regulations that freight forwarders big and small needed to satisfy. Even the most mundane goods, like salt shakers, required more documentation and licensing when transported into and out of the country. "Regulatory compliance was being outsourced to us. That was now a part of our value proposition, and it was difficult to keep up. Oh, and one more thing—the consequences of screwing up were *criminal*."

By 2005, the business was still on shaky ground. Although the need for capital investments was easing, competition from larger players was driving margins down. First Standard's annual revenues had grown to about $20 million, yet with most business founded on personal relationships with a few important customers, the firm still seemed fragile, vulnerable to the whims of its largest customers. Burdened by the need to make a $600,000 payroll every month, Shelley found himself feeling confused and increasingly frustrated. When would the firm's position stabilize? What business strategy would make that happen? Was he doing something wrong?

"Gets lonely at the top," Shelley remarks. "I'm hearing stuff from customers, but I don't know where to direct resources—to a Web server, to outsourcing? That's the spooky thing. I'm telling you, it's hard to compete right now—really, really hard."

As Shelley's story illustrates, rapid growth never comes easily and is usually rife with dilemmas. Indeed, no matter how solid their business concepts might be, growth confronts entrepreneurs with challenges they never could have imagined when they first started out.

Perhaps you're leading a rapid-growth company. You're convinced of your firm's potential, yet, more than ever, you're confused. Although business was once booming, now momentum is slowing. New customers seem eager to buy what you're selling, yet you just can't get the people in your organization to support you as you make the commitments required to meet customer needs. Some of your key employees are exhausted and seem unhappy. The old rules no longer seem to work. *You feel like the business is too big to be small and too small to be big.* And you don't know what to do to make things better.

As the leader, you must act. So you grope for new rules, managing the firm reactively, minute by minute. You're working harder than ever before, yet seeing no improvements. What's going on here? What are you doing wrong? How do you keep it going?

If you're like so many entrepreneurs I've seen, you're answering these questions by feeling bad and blaming yourself. *"I'm* the problem," you're saying. "It's my personality. I just don't have what it takes to get the job done." Or perhaps you're blaming the firm's problems on a specific decision you made, or on your failure to anticipate larger industry trends.

Leading an emerging growth firm can be a trying experience, but the troubles entrepreneurs encounter are not fundamentally of their own making. Rather, they stem from external causes relating to the specific challenges of the No Man's Land transition. Just as teenagers pass through a period of pain and awkwardness to reach the relative stability of adulthood, so must rapidly growing firms tackle a series of difficult and potentially fatal challenges with which entrepreneurs themselves are unfamiliar.

Let me say it again: It isn't you. It's adolescence. Even Microsoft, Starbucks, and Google were teenagers once. They faced the same difficulties that you now do. And they survived.

This chapter offers a new way of thinking about the experience of growing a small company into a big one. It describes the difficulties facing emerging growth companies as real, tangible things—not figments of the entrepreneur's imagination. And it points the way toward solutions. As we shall see, the growth that leads a company into No Man's Land will not lead a company out of it. To survive this phase in a company's life cycle, entrepreneurs must step away from the day-to-day and subject their businesses to a rigorous, objective analysis. Only by gaining a more impersonal understanding of their firms' and their own strengths and weaknesses can entrepreneurs take the necessary strategic steps toward surmounting them.

CONCEPTUALIZING RAPID GROWTH

Rob Wight, cofounder, president, and CEO of Channel Intelligence, a fast-growing Florida tech company, has some intriguing ways of talking about a firm's growth from its start-up phase to the point where it becomes a significant, sustainable business enterprise. According to Wight, starting a company down the growth path is rather like exploring:

> You parachute onto an island, set up camp, and create a very comfortable place. Then you send out scouts. Many never return, but a few come back saying, "This is the path." So what you have to do is make a heroic decision to strike camp and burn it and say we will now go and never ever look back.

Wight has another metaphor that he uses to describe the perils of business growth. He observes that "growing companies are also like steep winding roads down a mountainside with sharp corners and no guardrails, and your object is to stay on the inside shoulder."

What I like about both of these descriptions is that they describe rapid growth in geographic terms, as treacherous territory—an uncharted island, a curvy road—that needs to be traversed. That's exactly how the hundreds, if not thousands, of entrepreneurs I've spoken to over the years have experienced it. To be sure, the specific images many of them fall back on are different—crossing the Sahara, for instance, or steering a ship through dangerous straits, or hiking through thick woods—but the basic idea of exploring difficult and disorienting terrain is echoed by entrepreneurs over and

over again. In fact, the idea of rapid growth as an extreme and perilous voyage of discovery has come up so many times, in so many different contexts, and in so many different industries, that I've created my own geographically oriented name for a firm's painful adolescence: No Man's Land.

The No Man's Land concept, and geographic metaphors in general, are powerful because they capture so many facets of the actual experience of steering a growth company. Exploration of dangerous and unknown territory is disorienting, and so is leading a firm through rapid growth. Both endeavors can be extremely lonely and anxiety-producing; like Christopher Columbus and other famous explorers, leaders of emerging growth companies don't just have their own welfare to worry about but the welfare of a whole group of loyal subordinates with families and commitments of their own as well. Finally, both endeavors involve an identity crisis. "What *am I*," the entrepreneur wonders, "the much celebrated discoverer of America, or simply a scrappy dreamer with a big idea? What will it mean to me if I succeed or fail?"

By now, you're probably saying, "No Man's Land sounds familiar, but how does thinking about things in this way help me? I don't have the time to breathe, let alone answer my e-mails or read this book. How could understanding No Man's Land possibly matter?"

Conceptualizing rapid growth as something real, a specific geographic terrain, is not merely an abstract intellectual exercise; rather, it provides a firm's leadership with a means of analyzing rapid growth, breaking it down, and ultimately managing it. At the end of this chapter, I'll introduce the four *M*s, a clear and simple framework for understanding the difficulties posed by rapid growth and for helping firms deal with them. For now, let's explore the logical implications of the No Man's Land paradigm and shed some much-needed light on the puzzling phenomenon of business growth.

Corollary #1: Rapid Growth Has a Clear Beginning

The first implication of the No Man's Land paradigm may seem obvious, yet it bears stating: Like any journey, passage through No Man's Land has a clear starting point. In some cases, this starting point involves a conscious decision on the part of the entrepreneur to traverse No Man's Land. As Wight puts it, the entrepreneur boldly resolves "to strike camp and burn it and say we will now go and never ever look back."

I should stress, however, that it hardly ever happens that way. The vast majority of entrepreneurs who enter No Man's Land—that period when a firm is too big to be small and too small to be big—do so unintentionally, without even realizing it. Committed to their ideas, these men and women jump in and go for growth without even knowing where they are ultimately headed. It's not like leaders of fast-growth companies show up for work on Monday and say, "Oh, my gosh, I'm in No Man's Land."

In fact, No Man's Land is dangerous precisely because it's like getting lost in the wilderness: The unknown terrain comes on subtly, gradually, almost imperceptibly. When the entrepreneur finally realizes something is seriously wrong, often it is too late. And the process of grappling with its challenges can be so frustrating. How do you respond to something you only vaguely understand? As Wight says, "Just showing up the next morning is in many cases the key to the fight. It's excruciating, but you simply have to show up."

When I first describe No Man's Land in my seminars, audience members are typically stunned and hit by a mix of emotions. They experience relief at discovering that their problems are not inherently of their own making, but they also feel an overwhelming sense of guilt—the idea that as responsible leaders of a company *they should have known*. Some entrepreneurs literally shrink in their seats. "It's embarrassing," they say. "You're talking about *me*."

If you're feeling bad about getting caught in No Man's Land, you need to remember that you are going through a phase that every firm and every leader must traverse. As a leader of an emerging growth business, you are probably so busy managing increasingly complex day-to-day operations that you don't even register the firm's passage into a fundamentally new and different place. You are not a poor leader; you are simply overwhelmed by realities that are not obvious, that nobody told you about, that you have no experience dealing with, and that are difficult even to put into words.

Corollary #2: Growth Confronts Companies with Common Problems

As a distinct piece of geography, No Man's Land looks more or less the same to all who pass through it. In particular, the set of business problems confronting a company's leadership in No Man's Land include the following:

- The firm has difficulty fulfilling the customer promises it has to make in order to keep growing.
- Business decisions become increasingly complex and beyond the capacity of existing leadership to handle intuitively.
- The firm lacks a sense of how it is making money and what its future profitability picture will look like.
- The capital markets are closed, and the firm has difficulty obtaining the financing it needs.
- The firm's leadership feels stuck and stagnant.
- Reporting systems no longer provide meaningful information about the business.

Over time, these distinct problems give rise to a broader sense of vertigo and puzzlement experienced by many leaders of growth companies. The entrepreneur feels that he or she is losing control; that the tried-and-true rules don't work anymore; that the firm's basic vision is still right, but employees are having trouble keeping up. Does any of this sound familiar?

Corollary #3: There Is No Shortcut through Rapid Growth

Say you're Lewis and Clark and you're trying to reach the Pacific during the early nineteenth century. You can't simply hop on a plane to finish the journey when the going gets tough, nor can you have the crew of the *Enterprise* beam you up. You have only two choices for survival: either go back to the safety of the starting point, or push forward armed with some new way of handling the challenges before you.

No Man's Land confronts entrepreneurs with a similar quandary. This is the wilderness we're talking about here. A firm can't survive for very long while standing in one place. Remember the statistics: If the entrepreneur doesn't somehow find a way to get through No Man's Land, the firm will eventually go back or go under. It's that simple.

Of course, companies differ in exactly how long it takes to pass through adolescence. In the case of the national restaurant chain Noodles & Company, No Man's Land lasted a couple of years, ending only when the company found experienced leadership to complement the founders' own significant branding expertise. Since then the company has sustained further dramatic growth. For PATLive, a Florida-based telephone answering service, passage through adolescence lasted a full five years. The ability of PATLive's founder, Glen Davidson, to remain in limbo for so long with an insufficient executive team reflected the specific strengths of his original business model.

Like any voyage of discovery, a trip through No Man's Land is painful and transformative. To make it through, you've got to tackle its challenges head-on—the more quickly and efficiently, the better.

Corollary #4: On the Other Hand, No Man's Land Happens Only Once

The trip through No Man's Land is a unique transition that happens early in a firm's life cycle. Like human adolescence, it represents a developmental bridge between being small and being big. Once you've passed through the awkwardness, however, you're done. You've made it through.

To say that firms enter No Man's Land early in their life cycles does not mean that they do so quickly after the firm's founding. Research has indicated that many firms operate for years as small businesses before circumstances, innovations, and intuition combine to kick a company into growth mode. Pate Dawson, a food distributor based in Goldsboro, North Carolina, was a fairly small family business for more than a hundred years before Mac Sullivan took over in the early 1990s from his uncle and father. Making important alterations to the firm's model, Sullivan has increased the firm's revenue fifteen-fold over the past fifteen years, to a quarter billion dollars. Likewise, Heritage Information Systems was for a decade a small-scale consulting firm built around its founder's unique talents. During that time, the firm performed computerized audits of pharmacies on behalf of insurance companies. In 2001, Heritage began selling a software product that helped pharmacies gain Medicaid authorization before filling prescriptions, and for the next four years the firm experienced explosive growth.

To assert that firms traverse No Man's Land only once does not mean that they thereafter enjoy smooth sailing for the rest of their life cycles. On the contrary: After No Man's Land, the typical company can expect to realign its business substantially every three to four years. At each of these points, the firm makes some big bets, deciding which customers to make promises to so as to continue along the growth trajectory.

Consider, for instance, the case of Goldman Sachs, one of the nation's oldest investment banking firms. Responding to the requests of existing customers, Goldman Sachs began offering new financial instruments, such as swaps and derivatives, that allowed its customers to manage risk better. Servicing these new risk-management offerings in turn forced Goldman Sachs to transform its organization and to invest heavily in a proprietary trading system. Such wrenching change has paid off: Goldman Sachs recently achieved a record 40 percent quarterly return on equity, and is now paying an average compensation of $520,000 to its staff of twenty-four thousand.[11]

As anyone who's had teenagers knows, growing pains are difficult to endure, but they impart lessons that will serve your children for the rest of their lives. It's the same with a growth firm traversing No Man's Land. You embark on the journey, and it's tough, but if the journey doesn't kill you, you will eventually reach a point where your company has the tools to keep growing through future transitions. These tools include:

- **A brand:** After No Man's Land, the marketplace has confidence in your company. Customers associate your company's name with a known value proposition and turn to your firm first to fill their needs. Your brand not only gives you the benefit of the doubt in relation to competitors; it also leads customers to invite you to develop on their behalf the very new products and services you will need to continue along the growth trajectory.

- **A proven and profitable value proposition:** As we'll see in chapter 2, passage through No Man's Land forces your firm to identify and nurture a core set of deliverables, either as a product or a service or a combination of both. The marketplace has applauded your firm by deciding that these deliverables are worth paying for, above and beyond your business's cost structure.

- **A distinct culture:** By successfully transforming its business, your firm has demonstrated its ability to make the right bets and to assimilate new ideas and perspectives. As a result, your company's constituencies, including vendors and employees, have come to trust in your leadership team's decision-making ability. As we'll see in chapter 6, this process of decision making itself gives rise to a distinct culture within the firm, one that propels the firm to greater and greater growth.

We can summarize by saying that No Man's Land, the first, seminal transition, leaves firms with a "corporate character" upon which they can draw when confronting subsequent transitions. A company that has passed through No Man's Land has achieved some measure of stability. There are still serious challenges, but the firm's survival is no longer in jeopardy. There are more levers to pull and more resources to call upon. The firm will be around for a while, and everyone knows it.

Most of all, the entrepreneur knows it. It's clear to the entrepreneur that the firm can survive outside of his or her own personal efforts. The momentum of the business is now self-generating, and there is less risk. As a result, it's more fun again to come to work. The burden has been lifted and the entrepreneur has the luxury of taking on a long-term *investor's* perspective rather than that of an operator in survival mode.

Corollary #5: Rapid Growth Has a Clear Endgame

Just as a journey leads you to a specific geographical locale, so the growth process leads a firm to one of several possible outcomes. Confronted by the challenges of No Man's Land, firms will either:

- Continue to function as a smaller firm organized to leverage the entrepreneur's own unique abilities. Firms that follow this path typically nurture close personal relationships with customers, becoming "small giants," that is, companies that "choose to be great instead of big."*

---

*Burlingham, *Small Giants*. For a concise summary of the book's main ideas, see Burlingham, "There Is a Choice," *Inc.* (February 2006): 81. Page xiii of Burlingham's book offers a fuller description of "small giants": Aside from earning "a good return on their investment," these companies are "also interested in being great at what they do, creating a great

- Continue to grow, evolving into a firm that dramatically changes its marketplace or defines a new one.[12]
- Be acquired by a larger company. As we shall see in chapter 8, firms that follow this path become the research and development arms of large corporations, and in this way make a real contribution to those companies' ability to remain innovative.
- Get stuck in the transition and go out of business.

With the exception of the last possibility, each of the outcomes listed above has its pros and cons. This book is designed to help entrepreneurs determine which destination is right for them, factoring in the entrepreneurs' values, their personalities, and the constraints of their businesses. For now, let me simply affirm that *all* emerging growth firms face a basic choice among these options, even family-owned firms. Leaders of family-owned businesses often want to pass on their firms to future generations, and I applaud that, but they, too, must decide whether they should stay small, grow into a much larger firm, or sell if they are not to go out of business.

SO HOW DO I GET THROUGH NO MAN'S LAND?

Let me put the question back to you. If you're an entrepreneur trying to make your way through forbidding and unknown terrain, what do you need? Three things: a map, a high place from which to orient yourself, and navigational rules to help you determine your position on the map as you move forward. Fortunately, these tools are here in this book for the taking. The next four chapters provide you with the map and the navigational rules, while the book as

---

place to work, providing great service to customers, having great relationships with their suppliers, making great contributions to the communities they live and work in, and finding great ways to lead their lives. They've learned, moreover, that to excel in all those things, they have to keep ownership and control inside the company and, in many cases, place significant limits on how much and how fast they grow."

a whole provides you with an opportunity to gain a strategic perspective on your business, its processes, and the challenges before it.

In this chapter, I've used the No Man's Land concept to help bring to light a phenomenon—a transition unique in a company's history—that has until now been murky and poorly understood. The next four chapters take this a step further. They "map" the No Man's Land phenomenon by breaking it down into four distinct parts: Market, Management, Model, and Money. Analysis of this map in turn gives rise to a set of four rules for navigating a firm through No Man's Land. Not only do these rules work, they hold true irrespective of the firm's specific challenges and the industry in which it competes. Together, the "map" and the navigational rules give entrepreneurs a good portion of what they need to see their firms safely through the potentially fatal dangers that confront them during their transitions.

Some if not all of the navigational rules might seem counterintuitive, puzzling, or even downright disturbing. This is, strangely enough, as it should be. Think about it: When you fly an airplane in rough weather, you get vertigo. You can't fly on the basis of how you feel, but rather on the basis of what your instruments tell you. Likewise, in taking a firm through No Mans' Land, you're essentially flying blind. To make it to the other side, you need to execute the navigational rules regardless of how you feel, even if the rules are counterintuitive. They are your instruments, the only things between you and a fiery death.

So much for the map and the navigational rules. To make proper use of them, you have to first know where you are; only in this way can you come up with a viable plan for future action. In other words, you need to wrench yourself out of the day-to-day and bring yourself to a high place from which to become strategic and apply the map to your own situation.

Stepping away from the day-to-day might itself seem counterintuitive at a time when the demands on your time appear greater than ever. But trust me, it's necessary; otherwise the other tools I'm providing are useless.

Retreating to a high place from which you can survey the landscape shouldn't be all that foreign to you. At your company's birth, you didn't have a set of complex instruments at your disposal with which to micromanage day-to-day challenges. All you had was a business idea and the will to succeed. In effect, you were standing outside your industry looking in, and although from this vantage point you didn't know many of the specifics, you did have the opportunity to evaluate your firm more broadly, more strategically.

Your task now in getting through No Man's Land is to recover something of this original strategic vision. You need to forget about all the tiresome details and subject yourself and the business to a rigorous, objective analysis. You need to ask the "why" questions, not merely the "how" questions: Why would a customer want to do business with me? Why am I in this business to begin with? Why is it so important that I grow?

As a practical matter, there are as many ways to step away from the day-to-day as there are entrepreneurs. I like to smoke what I call "a long cigar" to think things through. Burt Prater, the entrepreneur we met in the introduction, was so insanely busy growing his firm that the only way he could find time to think was to book a first-class flight across the country. When he got off the plane, he immediately boarded another plane and flew right back—for the sole purpose of enjoying more time without distractions.

This book is designed to spur and guide you in your efforts to gain perspective on your business. The chapters that follow do not merely inform you about No Man's Land but also give you a series of unique opportunities to step away and get strategic. Sprinkled throughout you'll find exercises and questions designed to get you thinking about specific areas of your business, down to the next e-mail you need to send, the next phone call you need to make. Moreover, the next four chapters are ordered as a progressive intellectual exercise designed to help you think more and more deeply about the big challenges facing your firm. So sit back, light that cigar—we've got some thinking to do.

2

Market Misalignment

Growing out of touch with customer needs—or "market misalignment"—is the most fundamental peril facing firms in No Man's Land. In its early stages, a firm grows on the strength of a simple, nonfiltered exchange between the customer and a single point of contact, the entrepreneur. The entrepreneur decides which promises to make to which customers and simultaneously changes the firm's operations to meet those promises. It's an exciting process of experimentation and innovation that drives the firm forward and leads it to develop a defining value proposition. Rapid growth, however, intensifies the demands on the entrepreneur, rendering him or her physically unable to monitor and adapt the firm to changing customer needs. A gap opens between the promises made to customers and the operations required to satisfy them. As the entrepreneur struggles to do everything at once, simplicity no longer characterizes the customer-firm interface. The company loses its competitive edge, momentum falters, and sales stagnate.

THE BIRTH OF INNOVATION

When Judy Starkey founded Chamberlin Edmonds in 1986, she didn't have extensive capital or a long line of customers or even a formal business plan. She did, however, have a sound idea. From her work as a government medical benefits administrator, Starkey knew that a sizable percentage of government benefits went unclaimed because indigent patients and the hospitals that served them couldn't navigate the maddening complexities of Social Security, Medicare, and other programs. By helping hospitals to identify eligible patients, and by helping patients to fill out and submit government applications, Starkey thought she could secure benefits for these patients, thereby enhancing the revenue streams of client hospitals.

Starkey's first months in business were tough. To service her first client, a hospital in south Georgia, she was forced to separate from her family and relocate three hours away. While she was still adjusting to this situation, she was confronted with a number of pressing business issues, including an untrustworthy and unreliable business partner and the emergence of executives within the client hospital who were opposed to her work. Cash flow was also a huge problem. Although Chamberlin Edmonds claimed a percentage of all benefits recovered for the hospital, the slow pace of government benefits administration meant that Starkey had to wait an average of nine to ten months from the time she took on a patient's case until the time she would receive compensation. As a result, cash was so short that she had to borrow $150 just to put on Christmas for her family.

Starkey persevered. She had little choice: Her adopted son was autistic and required expensive, round-the-clock supervision. "Failure in my case was not an option," Starkey reports. "I had my child's welfare resting squarely on my shoulders. When I started this business, I sat down and told myself that I absolutely, positively would not fail. I was excited to be in business but also really, really scared."

Starkey didn't fail. By the early 1990s, she had created an impressive track record, retrieving benefits for a stunning 94 percent of patients referred to her. Her client list had grown, as had her employee roster.

Why was Starkey so successful early on? The answer is simple: alignment with customer needs.

Businesses exist to meet customer needs, or, in other words, to provide *value*. **Indeed, the profit a firm generates can be viewed as nothing other than the customer's applause for the value a firm creates over its cost structure.** In most emerging growth companies, a sustainable value proposition derives from the high-performance, cheap, and innovative labor of the entrepreneur and his or her core group of partners or employees. Certainly some of these companies have breakthrough products or services, but such offerings have been developed thanks to the complete dedication of entrepreneurs and their teams. The entrepreneur makes promises to meet customer needs—often on the basis of the entrepreneur's own talents or ideas—and the business in turn functions as a series of resources designed to support these promises. Over time, iterations of

Market alignment is obtained when a business consistently delivers a compelling value proposition in a simple exchange.

Alignment

Company is small
and entrepreneur
is in control

The Business

Simplicity

Customer

this process managed by the entrepreneur and his or her core team shape and refine the innovative value proposition.

In the case of Chamberlin Edmonds, Starkey added value for hospitals by successfully coordinating the needs of three very different constituencies: government agencies, hospitals, and indigent patients. Hospitals had little knowledge of the byzantine rules that governed federal and state programs; they didn't even know how to bill agencies for services rendered once access to benefits had been obtained. At the same time, hospitals possessed neither the manpower nor the expertise to interview indigent patients. They were therefore unable to extract the information they needed to identify eligible patients and file successful benefits claims. Indigent patients, meanwhile, did not possess the knowledge, the expertise, or the resources to represent their cases to either the hospital or government agencies.

As a former government employee, Starkey possessed the knowledge and contacts necessary to deal with tough Social Security and Medicaid regulations. What surprised her, though, was that she also had a knack for dealing effectively and compassionately with indigent and uninsured patients.

To assess a patient's eligibility for benefits, Starkey probed deeply into patients' lives, asking questions about their medical and work histories, their living situations, their personal relationships, and their assets. As Starkey soon realized, success in this critical task meant, above all, treating patients with dignity and respect. "In this business, it's the little things that matter," Starkey says. "For example, when I first started out, I never would wear jeans to interview patients in a hospital. Even today, I insist that all of our employees dress well and handle themselves professionally. And that's only the beginning. In my world, if you're rude to a patient, you're out of here the same day, no exceptions."

Just as important as Starkey's ability to deliver on hospitals' and patients' needs, though, was her ability to identify those needs in the first place. In both personal and professional capacities, Starkey had dealt with the medical-benefits recovery process long enough to know it inside and out. She had developed an intuitive understanding of what patients and hospital administrators were like, and what they needed. This knowledge, coupled with her own unique skills and her willingness to immerse herself in the details of patients' cases, comprised Chamberlin Edmonds's innovative value proposition. From the moment the firm opened its doors, its customers got this undiluted value proposition directly managed by the founder herself in a simple exchange.

MAINTAINING ALIGNMENT

Of course, it's one thing to be aligned, quite another to *stay* aligned. During the firm's early stages, the entrepreneur instinctively manages development of the value proposition by deciding which promises to make to which customers, then changing the business incrementally to meet those promises. The right promises lead to development of the firm's ultimate value proposition and to innovations that will continue to drive the company's sales.

Leaders of successful start-ups are able to deliver value precisely because they are attuned to even minuscule changes in the needs of their customers. With the business still small and the number of customers few, entrepreneurs play a key role in delivering relevant products or services, and as a result become familiar with customer needs firsthand. The perpetual conflict between operations and customer-driven innovation is handled during a firm's formative stages; entrepreneurs undertake both of these functions in a continuous, organic way.

In the early days of Chamberlin Edmonds, for instance, Starkey herself did much of the grunt work, crisscrossing Georgia to visit desperately ill patients in their homes and hospital beds. "I've truly seen and done it all," Starkey says. "I've literally had to drag an alcoholic patient out of a gin still to attend his benefits hearing. I've gone to the rural homes of psychiatric patients, interviewing violent people without an escort. In one of my earliest cases, I helped out a woman who lived on a struggling Georgia farm. Her name was

Sylvia, and she was really sick with diabetes. After several visits, we calculated that she and her family qualified for government benefits, but just barely. And then I saw a huge pregnant sow snorting around the yard. I nearly had a heart attack. 'How much is that pig worth?' I asked. When she told me, I informed her that she would need to kill the pig, or else she wouldn't qualify for benefits. And that's what she did. She killed the pig."

Sometimes the outcomes weren't so happy. In one case, Starkey worked with a long-distance truck driver who had a rare heart condition and needed a transplant. "For eight years he had been denied benefits," Starkey recalls. "We not only won him the benefits, but also got the government to come up with the back payments." In advance of the check's arrival, Starkey warned the man that he could expect a large sum of money. " 'You know,' I said, 'you're going to have to prepare yourself for this. You'll receive a ton of money. You'll be able to buy a house for your family and live very comfortably.' A few weeks later, a check for ninety thousand dollars arrived. When the man opened it, he had a heart attack on the spot. The good news actually killed him."

Thanks to such grass-roots contact with patients and hospitals, Starkey was able not only to register slight changes in customer needs but also to quickly shift the business to respond to them. In fact, most successful emerging growth companies are nimble in this way; entrepreneurs have the ability to line up the resources necessary to meet customer commitments almost instantaneously, and as a result they offer their customers the benefits of a simple and relatively easy commercial exchange, all the while defining the firm's ultimate value proposition. In larger, more bureaucratic companies, the internal change necessary for maintaining alignment occurs slowly, making such companies relatively complex to do business with. Like me, a number of you reading this book have worked in large companies. How much time did we spend in meetings trying to get the company's organizational structure caught up with what we knew our customers needed?

Reality Check

Is my company simple to do business with?

MAINTAINING ALIGNMENT:
THE KEY TO INNOVATION

Over time, the ongoing, iterative efforts at maintaining market alignment spur profound evolution and innovation within the firm. For instance, if you ask a given entrepreneur why his or her company is international in scope, do you know what they'll say? "A customer asked us to do something international, so we became international." More broadly, if you ask how a particular innovation came about, the entrepreneur will relate how the firm was trying to solve a particular client problem and did not realize that in the process they were innovating for a whole group of future customers.

That's typically the way it works: Customers ask for new products or services that require substantial changes to the business, or, alternately, they introduce your company to new customers who require new commitments. These commitments in turn alter the business and ultimately define a core set of expertise, abilities, and innovations that make up the company's value proposition. Make one set of promises and the firm will evolve in a certain direction to meet them. Make another set, and the firm will look very different as time passes. In making opportunistic promises to customers, growth firms become living laboratories given over to a process of discovering what ultimately is the right product, service, and target customer.

The changes that accrue as a result of a firm's drive to maintain alignment can sometimes lead to profound organizational shifts. My firm started off by providing emerging growth companies with part-time CFOs. Our growing clients took on private equity, and as private equity firms became familiar with our services, they wanted our partners to serve as permanent co-employed executive leaders in companies. They also wanted us to provide technology leadership services. More recently, customers have asked us to augment these leadership services with support staff such as controllers and subject matter experts. In effect, our customers desire full-scale consulting teams capable of solving specific problems, under the banner of resources that enhance the company's financial and technology leadership. So we had to figure out a way to accommodate that paradigm. Today we have a whole new customer base, and we are serving it in ways we never could have imagined.

Sometimes a promise made to a single client or group of clients—"marquee customers," as David G. Thomson calls them[13]—triggers a chain reaction that supports a firm's entire growth and innovation. During the 1990s, the food distributor Pate Dawson made its money selling to independent restaurants and handling food procurement for local school districts. In 2003, however, the firm had a chance to win the account of a restaurant chain with 300 locations. To serve this one customer, Pate Dawson had to enhance its infrastructure dramatically. Thinking of how to leverage this investment led Mac Sullivan, Pate Dawson's president, to develop a whole new model for servicing the independent restaurant businesses it found on the routes it had established to serve the large restaurant chain.

Whereas traditional food distributors compensate salespeople according to their margins, forcing restaurant owners to bid each product among multiple food service providers in order to ensure competitive pricing, Mac saw the opportunity to take a more transparent, partnership approach. Putting his own big-chain resources and economies of scale to use, Mac designed a program whereby his company promised to work with the restaurant owners to rationalize their ordering so as to achieve a targeted food-cost percentage. In exchange, the restaurant would agree to make Pate Dawson its exclusive buying representative. By securing virtually all of an individual restaurant's business, Mac tripled his revenue per stop, creating efficiencies that in turn allowed him to make the customer promise that forms the basis of this new, innovative value proposition. In this way, Pate Dawson is innovating a new value proposition in one of the most seemingly staid and noncreative industries there is—all because of one customer promise.

The process of internal change spurred by the drive to maintain alignment is organic. It occurs so quickly and seamlessly that often even the leader of a gazelle isn't fully conscious of it. I typically liken the entrepreneur's awareness of a firm's growth to the way a parent views his own growing child. Parents observe their children so often that they frequently don't realize just how rapidly they are changing, even though such change is easily recognizable to an outside visitor. Only when the visitor points it out do the parents say, "Holy moly, you're right, I had no idea!"

If the process of maintaining market alignment spurs internal evolution and innovation, it also serves as a key driver of a firm's overall growth. During the 1990s, Pate Dawson was a $25 million company; today the firm is a *$225 million* company, and growing faster than the industry, largely because of new promises made to customers and the consequent evolution in the firm's value proposition.

It is so important to decide carefully which promises to extend to which customers. The correct decisions will keep you growing through No Man's Land, while the wrong ones will kill you. An entrepreneur might make some promises that lead to stadiums full of new customers, whereas others might lead to dead ends, tangling up the company with promises meaningful to only a few clients or cus-

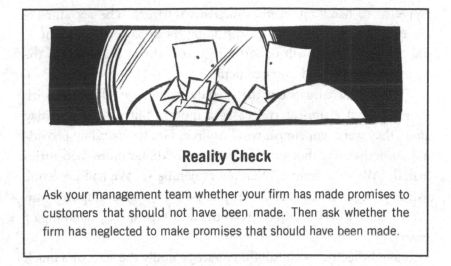

Reality Check

Ask your management team whether your firm has made promises to customers that should not have been made. Then ask whether the firm has neglected to make promises that should have been made.

tomers. The key is for you as the leader to make the right decisions that lead to a growing and profitable customer base.

Deciding which promises to make to which customers is strategic planning in its essence. The decisions entrepreneurs make in maintaining alignment can shape their firms' fortunes for years to come. In his landmark book *Management: Tasks, Responsibilities, Practices*, Peter Drucker argues that strategy is essentially a forward-looking process whereby the manager strives to see around the corner and speculate about what the future might hold. "Management," he writes, "has no choice but to anticipate the future, to attempt to mold it, and to balance short range and long range goals." In this respect, strategy is inherently entrepreneurial, and indeed Drucker has an entire chapter titled "Strategic Planning: The Entrepreneurial Skill."[14]

MARKET MISALIGNMENT: A NATURAL OUTCOME OF GROWTH

In 1995, Chamberlin Edmonds won its biggest account ever when Grady Memorial Hospital, the largest trauma center in the Southeast, tapped it to handle its medical-benefits recovery. The account required a doubling of Chamberlin Edmonds's employees overnight. It was a wonderful growth opportunity, yet it thrust Starkey into the wrenching problem of misalignment.

Starkey had anticipated that Grady would provide them with four hundred claim-referral cases a month, but on the first day alone they were sent almost two hundred. Grady wound up providing more than one thousand referrals a month, far more than anticipated. "We were frantic," Starkey remembers. "We had everyone working nights, weekends. We put new employee training into overdrive. We even set up contests to encourage speedy handling of cases."

Such difficulties with fulfillment are typically the start of a much deeper problem: the inability to keep pace with customer needs. As your customer commitments increase, your personal synthesis of the marketing and operations functions breaks down. Demands placed on you create a situation where you physically cannot monitor and respond to customer needs. As you lose control, you make promises you cannot fulfill and grow increasingly oblivious to important market changes.

I am always amazed at how high the pain threshold is among entrepreneurs. These leaders can push themselves way beyond what most ordinary humans can tolerate. At some point, however, surging customer demand will exceed even the entrepreneur's physical limitations. The entrepreneur stops spending as much time with customers, and is no longer able to know firsthand the nuances of their needs. The promises he makes—his product and service offerings— might end up reflecting his personal desire to innovate rather than the customers' changing needs. Actual customer needs go unmet and the business as a whole loses momentum. If the firm cannot deliver beyond the entrepreneur's personal abilities, sales will inevitably slow. In this way, market misalignment is a natural and inevitable result of growth. To beat it, entrepreneurs have to realign their firms with the requirements of their markets.

The Superhuman Entrepreneur

If you're used to rapid growth and the rush of running a business that enjoys high-flying momentum, the stress of market misalignment will be especially difficult. Remember the feelings of vertigo and loss of control described in the last chapter? Here is where they flare up most intensely. You're working as hard as you can, yet because the business is misaligned, you're getting nowhere. The work itself becomes less and less attractive: Instead of focusing your efforts on building satisfying customer relations, you spend much of your time performing damage control for customer promises that were made but not kept.

On a more fundamental level, market misalignment is challenging because it confronts entrepreneurs with an identity crisis. A multitude of tempting potential customers appears on the horizon, but because entrepreneurs are so consumed with the task of putting out fires, they no longer have the bandwidth to consider which customers will open doors for the firm down the line and which won't. The promises the firm should be making are unclear, and as a result it is unclear where the company should be directing scarce resources. What exactly is the company all about? What differentiates the company from competitors in customers' minds? Having lost sight of this, entrepreneurs grow scared, and they frequently experience a crisis of confidence.

As entrepreneurs struggle with the firm's identity, they tend to curl up and become internally focused. One of the most dangerous reactions I have witnessed is the tendency for entrepreneurs to fall back almost exclusively on new product development as a way to recreate the growth experience they encountered before the company entered No Man's Land. "Now, wait a minute," you say, "I thought this whole growth process is about new product development and innovation." It surely is, but there is a huge difference between capturing, institutionalizing, and evolving the firm's core value proposition

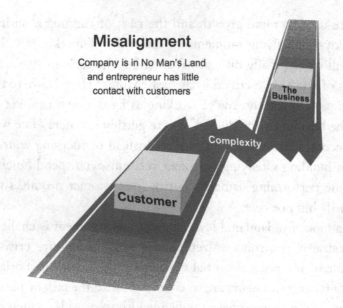

Misalignment

Company is in No Man's Land
and entrepreneur has little
contact with customers

The Business

Complexity

Customer

as a customer base changes and trying to solve all the company's problems with a new idea created from scratch. Remember, *boredom with the hard work of systematizing the core business has killed a whole lot of companies.*

Entrepreneurs are by nature creative, innovative people. As they grapple with market misalignment, they find it tempting to walk away from the hard work of institutionalizing their own ability to make and meet the right customer promises, and instead immerse themselves in the more gratifying work of developing something new from scratch. In the end, though, firms can't invent their way out of market misalignment. It would be nice if they could, but that's not how it works. Don't let boredom with the task of keeping the firm in alignment kill your company.

Signs That Your Company
Is Misaligned with the Market

- Has sales growth stalled?
- Do you feel you are losing your competitive advantage?
- Have tensions arisen between promises made (sales) and delivery (operations)?
- Are quality problems becoming more pressing? Are customer complaints mounting? Do you find yourself dealing with the miscues, not with high-touch (i.e., direct contact) customer relationshipbuilding?
- Are you becoming bored and frustrated to the point where you are turning to new product development as an escape?
- As you peruse your customer portfolio, are you unable to distinguish between "good" customers who will lead you to further growth and "bad" ones who won't?

SO HOW DO I BEAT
MARKET MISALIGNMENT?

There is only one sure way that I know of to identify the firm's real value proposition and regain alignment:

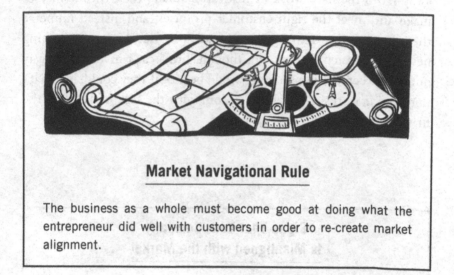

Market Navigational Rule

The business as a whole must become good at doing what the entrepreneur did well with customers in order to re-create market alignment.

To exit No Man's Land, firms need to surpass the entrepreneur's physical limitations by *institutionally* capturing the value proposition that has been developed through the entrepreneur's unique insights; in other words, they must re-create the initial synthesis between operations and marketing, maturing the value proposition by making use of employees and processes rather than one person's effort. They must create a means to sustain alignment that will continue to work even as the company scales upward.

Getting the business good at what the entrepreneur did well with customers is essentially a two-step process. First, entrepreneurs need to identify what exactly it was that they were good at. As we've seen, companies in misalignment are befuddled and scattershot;

their leaders are so overwhelmed with trying to meet disparate and perhaps inconsistent customer promises that they don't have a grip on what the company is all about, i.e., the core value proposition. To get out of No Man's Land, entrepreneurs need to dredge the company out of this identity crisis. Recognizing that the company cannot be all things to all customers, entrepreneurs need to isolate and identify their company's core competitive advantages and its sustainable value proposition. What was the definitive value proposition that led to the venture's growth in the first place? What made the company so unique and exciting to customers during the heady early days? Confronted with numerous market opportunities, entrepreneurs need to ask: Who are the *right* customers to extend promises to going forward?

A man once came up to me after a No Man's Land presentation and told me that he was in the used-aircraft-parts business. In four to five years, his firm grew its revenues from zero to $70 million. Now, though, sales were stagnant and he was no longer sure about what he needed to do to serve customer needs. The firm had fallen into misalignment.

"Well, what are you good at?" I asked.

He thought about it and said, "You know, it comes down to one thing: I know how to buy right. I have a sixth sense, an intuitive feeling, about what refurbished parts available to me on the market are good deals for my customers."

Bingo. What this entrepreneur was saying was that he was a parts trader with an instinctive ability to buy at a discount what he knew his customers would ultimately need. Earlier in the firm's history, he had spent time simultaneously with customers and with sellers, arbitraging between the two on a daily basis. "Buying right" became his core value proposition, without his ever fully realizing it. If this entrepreneur was to grow the company beyond its current size, he had to transfer this ability to the organization as a whole. Can you imagine what would happen if he tried to grow without doing so? Lacking an ability to "buy right," the firm would accumulate unsold inventory, lose profitability, and experience huge cash-flow problems.

Another way to describe identification of the core value proposition is to say that a firm needs to become more aware of its *brand*— what the brand is, and what it is not. A strong brand, after all, is not a logo or a tagline; rather, it reflects the firm's defining value proposition and customer expectations about this value proposition. When a firm gets mired in No Man's Land, its brand gets muddied, often as a result of the entrepreneur's indiscriminate acceptance of customer promises. I once asked a partner of mine who specializes in turn-around situations how often companies' prospects are thwarted by bad new ideas hung on otherwise good value propositions. His answer: "Every time."

As businesses expand, it's critical that entrepreneurs cultivate brand definition by testing every potential promise against the core value proposition. Once the firm is already in No Man's Land, however, the task becomes one of reconnecting with the brand, carving away what is nonessential.

Sam Norwood, a senior partner in our firm, uses a wonderful story to illustrate the necessity of reconnecting with the brand. His former mentor, the legendary businessman J. B. Fuqua, had purchased an old-line manufacturing firm in the Northeast. After spending a great deal of time performing due diligence, he believed that a radical shake-up was required to get the company to perform. Fuqua had directed the senior management team of the company to assemble and meet him for the first time in the boardroom, and to have every product that the company manufactured present on the table when he arrived. Fuqua also had a most peculiar request; he wanted the products to be put on the table in a very special manner, with the best-selling product at one end, the remaining products placed in descending order based on sales, and the lowest-selling product placed at the exact opposite end of the table from the best-selling product.

Fuqua entered the room. You can imagine what it looked like: an old, stately space with dark-wood paneling and a long table that stretched for miles. Fuqua's entrance, too, must have been quite a sight: This was the first time the management team had met Mr. Fuqua, and the tension must have been palpable. Upon receiving the customary introductions, Fuqua immediately turned to the CEO and asked which products, starting with the best seller, accounted for 80 percent of the company's revenues. The CEO, the VP of sales, and the CFO huddled for a few minutes, and then the VP of sales started with the best seller and counted back until he reached a product that he indicated was the proper cutoff point. Fuqua quietly walked over to that product, put his hand on the table, and proceeded to rake all the less-profitable products off the table and onto the laps of the team assembled around it. Pointing to the few products remaining on the table, Fuqua turned to the CEO and said, "By the end of the next quarter, these are the only products I want manufactured and sold by this company." Then he turned on his heel, left the room, and got on his jet to return to Atlanta.

Well, the company did exactly as Fuqua had directed. Sales immediately took off, generating increased earnings.

The second step for entrepreneurs, once the firm's identity crisis is dealt with, is to make the company good at what the entrepreneur

---

Working toward Realignment:
Three Epiphanies

- I do provide a unique value, and this is what I built my firm on.
- My clients and what I do for them have changed more than I ever thought they would.
- I can no longer keep the business physically aligned on the basis of my own efforts.

was initially good at, or, in other words, to systematize delivery of the value proposition. Entrepreneurs must create a series of *processes* that transform much of the work of delivering on customer promises into routine acts. One entrepreneur I know of has described this transformation in soccer terms. Early in a firm's history, the entrepreneur and his or her employees fulfill customer promises by pursuing a strategy akin to second-grade soccer, whereby everybody runs instinctively to the ball. To realign with customers and get through No Man's Land, a firm needs to create a system where everybody behaves rationally and plays a specific position. Only in this way can the firm hope to continue to win customers' hearts as the number of customers multiplies.

Consider the case of Chamberlin Edmonds. Once the short-term fires were extinguished, Starkey moved to find more permanent solutions to the problem of misalignment. Fortunately for her, she instinctively knew that she needed to systematize the firm's delivery of its value proposition. Specifically, the firm needed to institutionalize both the soft side of dealing with indigent patients and gaining their trust and the hard side of processing requests with impersonal bureaucratic government agencies. In effect, the company had to become good at what Judy herself was good at. "With Grady, I had to deal with process, process, process," Starkey recalls. "I knew that if we were to continue making money, we needed to migrate to a low-cost model without compromising patient interface."

By 1997, Chamberlin Edmonds had given all employees laptops and built a comprehensive software system that allowed for online processing of claims. The result was cleaner, better claims filing and lower overall labor costs. Shortly afterward, the firm systematized dealings with outpatient clients, creating a call center to handle their needs. During the 2000s, the firm has continued the task of systematization by using business process management technology to transform virtually every part of the business. As Starkey reflects, "We will never get completely away from our roots in high-touch, high-cost service delivery, but if we can implement low-cost, low-touch and medium-cost, medium-touch to the extent possible, we'll save a ton of money."

As a firm systematizes value delivery, it can set up processes to replicate the efforts, and in some cases the talents, of the original entrepreneur and his or her core team. These processes can fulfill many of the most vital functions, including acquiring customers, managing and retaining employees, tracking inventory, and identifying new needs for existing customers, to name but a few. Some processes can be completed using human means, as in the case of a

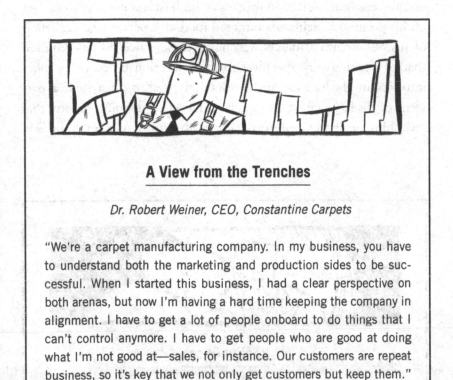

A View from the Trenches

Dr. Robert Weiner, CEO, Constantine Carpets

"We're a carpet manufacturing company. In my business, you have to understand both the marketing and production sides to be successful. When I started this business, I had a clear perspective on both arenas, but now I'm having a hard time keeping the company in alignment. I have to get a lot of people onboard to do things that I can't control anymore. I have to get people who are good at doing what I'm not good at—sales, for instance. Our customers are repeat business, so it's key that we not only get customers but keep them."

company that delivers a high-touch customer experience by setting up call centers and hiring highly trained customer representatives. Others can be set up using technology, such as equipment that allows for high-quality, mechanized fabrication of something that the firm used to do by hand. Likewise, some of the processes a firm needs to put in place are required in all businesses of a certain size (e.g., computerized billing), while others need to be tailor-made for the individual firm (e.g., a hotel chain's proprietary guest-registration software).

Developing processes that replicate the entrepreneur's talents becomes a huge part of a company's competitive advantage. At Pate Dawson, Mac Sullivan has had to completely change the sales, delivery, and customer-selection process of his business in order to deliver on his promise to achieve a targeted food-cost percentage on behalf of his restaurant customers. Changing these processes has required that he devise a very specific customer-selection process that takes into account the location of the restaurant itself, the distribution patterns of his large chain customer, and a set of defining criteria that gives him the confidence to take the customer on. As a result, he is in

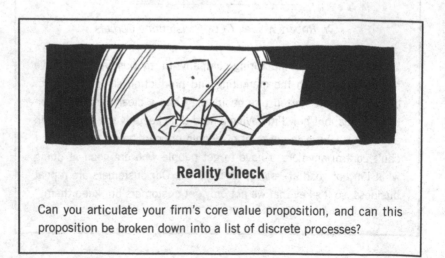

Reality Check

Can you articulate your firm's core value proposition, and can this proposition be broken down into a list of discrete processes?

a position to deliver an offering that even much larger competitors can't match.

In some situations, systematization of value delivery has the power to single-handedly and immediately transform a company. For more than a decade, Heritage Information Systems was essentially a consulting business whose core value proposition— effective detection of fraudulent insurance claims practices on the part of pharmacists—reflected the personal efforts and talents of its founder, John Tripodi, and a group of key employees. During the early 2000s, however, Heritage managed to systematize its industry and technical expertise by creating software products that performed new kinds of data-analysis tasks, such as prescription preauthorization and drug interaction detection. Revenues exploded, and within a few years Heritage had become not merely a different kind of company but an attractive target for acquisition by a larger competitor. Heritage was eventually sold for tens of millions of dollars.

Developing and implementing processes within a company is not always an easy task. Firms must often make wrenching changes to their internal structures that employees cannot understand. During the early 2000s, the Florida-based computer start-up Channel Intelligence spent two years developing a proprietary database technology that facilitates online retail transactions. When development was complete, the firm asked all its product development engineers to go into the market and discover promising customer applications for this technology. After a year, though, it became clear that the firm had become *too* customer-centric; by devoting all its resources to responding to requests from individual customers, Channel Intelligence had lost its ability to develop major iterations of its core technology. The solution was to split the engineering staff, having half deal with grass-roots client problems and half work more strategically to capture customer-generated innovations to its core technology. Unfortunately, implementing this structural change, and the processes associated with it, was highly unpopular. "Everybody hated it," Rob Wight, Channel's CEO, recalls. "These were very difficult times. We lost some good people. But we needed processes in hand to respond quickly to small-scale client needs while still doing the big technological things that would move the company forward over the long term. So change we did."

If systematization of the value proposition is critical, close concentration on the value proposition comprises the single most important thing a company can do as it grows. At an extreme, many firms dedicate themselves exclusively to the development of their core value proposition with no thought initially to its potential profitability.[15] When the Boulder, Colorado–based restaurant chain Noodles & Company was getting off the ground in the mid-1990s, the firm initially focused on developing the best product possible, without much concern for profitability. Then the firm passed through a period in which it made no money. Only at this point did Noodles & Company try to figure out a way to make money at scale. The firm's management did this by analyzing its value-delivery system step-by-step. For instance, they broke down the function of sautéing foods into four jobs, simplifying it enough so that even a low-wage high-school employee could learn one or two of these jobs in a single day. The result was dramatically improved profitability based on a scalable system for delivering value.

MEASURING SYSTEMATIZATION

There is one final step an entrepreneur needs to take when implementing the market navigational rule. It is not enough to set up processes in your firm; you also have to develop ways to *measure* the results of the processes. Early on in the life of firms, entrepreneurs are already integrating measurement into firm operations without even realizing it. They know that an offering is acceptable or a customer initiative is working because they are getting instant feedback via their contact with customers. Now, though, impersonal, system-wide means of getting feedback must be integrated into the process. Otherwise, firms are essentially flying blind in their attempts to align with customer needs.

To complete our sense of what it takes to beat market misalignment, and to focus specifically on the challenge of measurement, let's take a look at the story behind a successful chain of music stores.

Rock-and-roll musicians would seem to be the last people interested in breaking up business operations into a series of measurable, rule-bound processes. But are they really? Meet George Hines, a friendly, energetic man with streaks of gray in his hair. Hines started George's Music in 1977 for a simple reason: He wanted to create a place where anyone could buy a musical instrument and receive decent, respectful service. As an aspiring musician growing up in Philadelphia, Hines spent a lot of money on instruments, but was never treated well. "People used to talk down to me, look at me suspiciously, refuse to let me play the instruments—and I was the customer! When I was fourteen, I went into a store and they treated me okay. I tried to tip the salesman because he actually let me try a guitar. That's how bad it was."

George was still a student at Ursinus College, an hour west of Philadelphia, when he decided to do something about the problem. With little inventory beyond his personal guitar collection, he rented a space near the college, fixed it up, and started booking music lessons. On the first day of business, nobody came in, and the police ticketed his car. This was not the start George had hoped for, but business soon took off, spurred by word-of-mouth accounts of Hines's personal attention and dedication to musicians. Unlike other stores, Hines would display all the merchandise out on the floor, where musicians could try it, even if this exposed him to increased shrinkage. In fact, he had a rule in place: Nobody could play the instruments in the store *except* the customers. Hines treated musicians as if they were his best friends, and some repaid him by helping him unload products from the delivery truck. "We were on a mission from God," Hines recalls. "A cult grew up around the store, and this helped define our culture. It was an attitude. We were rebels with a cause, and people responded well to that."

After eight years in business, George's Music was established and profitable enough that Hines was contemplating expanding to a second location. The question he faced, though, was how to re-create on a broader scale the value proposition he was already delivering—respectful, friendly, and devoted customer service. More fundamentally, he was wondering how he would replicate the unique culture that had given rise to that customer service in the first place.

Rather than eschew systematization, Hines resolved to become almost fanatical in his drive to develop company-wide processes. Knowing that he would be relying on employees now rather than on his own personal attention, he devised checklists for even the most minute operations: how to open the store; what to do when the customer asked for a refund. He developed a detailed selling process which every employee had to accept, put together a formal training manual, and held training sessions for new employees in the basement of his first store. Hines also developed an effective hiring process, interviewing hundreds of people for a single position to ensure that those he hired were true believers in the business. Finally, Hines automated as many back-office processes as he could, enhancing service performance by computerizing in the early 1980s.

Hines's efforts paid off. The second store was a rousing success, and it was followed by two more in the Philadelphia area. Wishing to prove to himself that he had captured the value proposition, and that his processes could be controlled by the measurement systems, Hines decided to expand next to a distant market. In 1991, he discovered that Orlando, Florida, suffered from the same lack of friendly, musician-oriented stores that he had first encountered in Pennsylvania. Today he has six stores across Florida, and ten stores overall. Buoyed by this success, he has developed a musical instrument–buying consortium that represents almost 8 percent of the country's retail trade.

Critical to Hines's success was implementation of a rigorous measurement system. As Hines relates: "I do auditing in the stores, as well as mystery shops where someone shows up pretending to be a customer. I've also got fifteen key indicators for the business that I monitor every month. If there's a problem, I can dig in. I am excited by the quality of our service—I like to be better than everyone else. I'm more in control of the ten stores than I was of one." The business, in other words, is now good at what he initially had been good at.

If a rock-and-roll musician can develop processes and measurement systems to keep his business aligned with customers, then anyone can. Just click onto the George's Music Web site (www. georgesmusic.com), and you'll find that Hines remains as true as ever to his core value proposition. "Welcome to George's Music," the site reads. "This web site was created by musicians, for musicians. You will find everything you need to help you better enjoy your instrument . . ." Next to this proclamation is a picture of George Hines, smiling, encouraging others to partake of the joys of making music, just as he always has.

MARKET ALIGNMENT *M* PAUSE POINT

As we've seen, market misalignment comprises the most fundamental set of challenges facing companies in No Man's Land. An entrepreneur can lead his company through No Man's Land only if he can identify a value proposition that can be institutionalized within his business. Institutionalizing that value proposition means developing processes that allow the firm to deliver that core value and evolve it so that the firm remains aligned with ever-changing customer needs. There are many ways that firms can systematize value delivery—through a clearly defined customer interaction process, in the case of George's Music, or by separating out high-touch processes from the processes that can be automated, in the case of Chamberlin Edmonds. In each of these cases, the value was born out of a set of skills and passions held originally by the entrepreneur but ultimately captured by the business itself.

How exactly does a firm go about systematizing internal processes? The only way, ultimately, is by hiring experienced senior managers who have already learned how to build processes on somebody else's dime. Market alignment issues thus lead invariably to management issues, the subject of the next chapter. Before we go on to consider management issues, however, let's linger over the material in this chapter a bit longer.

If you're trying to lead a rapid-growth company through No Man's Land, the issues associated with the marketing M lie at the heart of the thinking you need to do to determine whether or not to continue growing your firm. If you can't get a handle on your core value proposition, or can't imagine a way to transfer its delivery to your firm as a whole, then you have some huge decisions to make. Rather than growing your firm, the path for you might be to stay small and optimize the business around your own personal talents and efforts. Take an honest look at your visions of growing a large enterprise and evaluate whether you might not be better off building what Bo Burlingham has termed a "small giant," a firm whose greatness lies in the quality it delivers rather than its size. Plenty of people in almost every industry create strong, sustainable businesses around their own expertise—and enjoy every minute of it. Let me be as direct as possible: It is ethical, legal, moral, and, in many cases, *good business* to stay small, make money, and enjoy the fruits of your personal talents and passions.

As we shall see, maintaining alignment is the most difficult problem a firm faces; management, model, and money issues are more concrete and straightforward compared to this. So do yourself a favor—think long and hard about the marketing M before moving on. Begin by trying to answer honestly the following questions: Where does my true passion lie in this business? Is the value I add something that can be systematized and infused into the organization as a whole? Then move on to the following pause point questionnaire.

Market Alignment Pause Point Questions

1. What are you, the entrepreneur, good at?
2. Does the business really offer anything unique, or is it just a service defined as your high-performance cheap labor?
3. What is really driving new product development? Is it based on an objective assessment of the promises that, once made, will lead you to future customers?
4. Are you bored with the day-to-day details of "cleaning up" the business after "messing it up" by making promises to customers?
5. Which customers would you bet on to lead you into the future, and which customers do you believe should be fired?
6. Name the one company that would be most interested in buying your company and explain why.
7. What do you have to do to ensure that your business can continue to deliver its value proposition in a simple exchange? What does your business have to do internally to keep it simple to do business with?

Don't keep these questions to yourself; challenge the organization and its constituencies to give you unfettered answers. For best results, shake up your inner circle and engage some folks whom you don't normally include in this type of exercise. Involve those folks in your business who have the most contact with customers, as well as those who deal with the day-to-day problems of missed expectations. Try posing these questions to your best or most promising customers. Although the ensuing discussion will quickly become extremely personal, stick with it—the insights gleaned could make the difference between your business's success and its failure.

3

Outgrowing Your Management

An entrepreneur can maintain alignment and ensure simplicity for customers when a company is small. However, once alignment is lost in a growing company, gaining it back requires experienced management and a control system that protects and enhances the firm's core value proposition. The entrepreneur must hire and delegate to senior management the responsibility of implementing and managing this control system. For many entrepreneurs, delegating constitutes the most personally challenging transition. Primarily, they fear losing control of a firm they've built from the ground up. Yet delegating to senior management is, in truth, the only way to gain back control. To make it through No Man's Land, a rapid-growth firm must complement the entrepreneur's vision and unique skills by injecting a healthy dose of new, experience-based expertise.

IN OVER OUR HEADS

When Glen Davidson founded PATLive, a telephone answering services company, in 1990, he had no inkling that the firm would become a rapid-growth company. He had been working at another company he had founded, giving motivational speeches to large sales staffs, and had realized that one of the firms' clients had no means of communication. He tried to talk the client into putting together a voice-mail communication system (e-mail didn't yet exist) and the client said, "You do it." So Glen Davidson hired some college kids, purchased some readily available technologies, and put together a voice-mail system. The client loved it, and a new company, PATLive, was born.

Success came fast and furious. After the first year, Davidson had ten employees, $400,000 in revenues, and gross margins of up to 80 percent. By 1998, the firm had grown to about $8 million in revenues, selling voice-mail systems to companies with far-flung networks of free-agent salespeople. PATLive made the *Inc.* 500 list of most rapidly growing companies three years in a row—in 1996, 1997, and 1998.

Then the firm stalled. One problem was the growing use of e-mail, which rendered PATLive's existing product obsolete. To adapt, Davidson added more value by injecting live operators into the automated voice system. He also added bells and whistles, such as the ability to transfer incoming calls to cell phones. The company remained extremely profitable, yet on a deep level, Davidson sensed that the firm had outgrown his interest in running the day-to-day operations. "My one true competency has always been my ability to listen to customers and to apply existing technology to their problems in a simple way," he explains. "What did I know about building systems? I knew I didn't want to be running this company as it grew—heck, I'm just a guy who loves fishing and frog gigging. I wanted to retire at fifty."

Davidson's initial attempts to hire professional management failed. Guided by a high-priced professional headhunter, he brought in an executive from a big voice technology firm in Atlanta with Amway as a customer. In short order, the executive went on to alienate Davidson, and, more important, to go after bad deals. "This was the heart of the problem. My strength was solving customer problems, but now this guy was in the way, deciding which customers to make promises to. I can't tell you how much this disrupted the firm." In 2004, Davidson reluctantly took back the reins. A year later, still wanting nothing more than to retire, he tried another executive. When that failed, he grew frustrated. "I was so sick and tired of the business. I felt that PATLive had outgrown me, and it showed. Our business was essentially stagnant between 2000 and 2004. Yet I just couldn't find the right person to drive the business."

Things finally changed in 2005, some seven to eight years after the firm first entered No Man's Land. Davidson hired an industry veteran who had been laid off by a technology firm, and the firm's fortunes improved almost instantaneously. Profits rose 100 percent and revenues 30 percent; 2006 promised to produce similar results. "It isn't just about the numbers," Davidson relates. "I *know* this is the right fit. The guy recognizes my talent when it comes to deciding which opportunities to go after. He's an operations man—he can't see around the corner like I can, and is happy to let me handle that. We meet regularly to discuss the business, and when we do I realize just how well we complement each other's strengths and weaknesses."

As Davidson's experience demonstrates, professional managers are often essential to a firm's successful navigation of No Man's Land. In transitioning through growth, most firms simply don't have the additional leadership experience they need to scale the business upward. As a result, the business stagnates—not just for lack of an understanding of where the business needs to go, but for a lack of the kind of expertise required to get it there.

As we saw in the last chapter, market realignment involves restoring simplicity into the business's customer-facing side. Yet paradoxically, such simplicity is achieved by making the back end more complex. A company realigning with its market is no longer a project that can be handled in an organic way by one person or even a few. Rather, the firm is on its way to becoming a sophisticated *organization* built around processes that any organization must have, in areas such as accounting, human resources, information technology, sales, and marketing. From a second-grade soccer team where everyone plays every position, the firm must evolve into a professional squad where people behave rationally and play specific positions.

Who should occupy these positions? As an entrepreneur in No Man's Land, you need competent and experienced people in leadership positions—people who can help you *execute*. After all, the firm is going through a transition without a ton of resources at its disposal; it can't make many mistakes and still hope to survive. What you as an entrepreneur are trying to do is akin to the driver who wishes to change the pistons of his car's engine while still driving the car at seventy miles per hour down a winding road. This tricky maneuver can be done, but to pull it off you'll need some people by your side who have already done it, and who have proven that they know what they are doing. Otherwise, your firm might wind up by the side of the road as a mangled, smoky wreck.

My mother used to say that if you take care of the little things in life, the larger obstacles you face will take care of themselves. In No Man's Land, the opposite holds true: The big things will sink you. If you don't have someone on staff who knows what your capital requirements will be one, two, or three years from now, and how to articulate those needs to the capital markets, you might run out of money just as you are on the verge of leaving No Man's Land. If you don't have someone adept at the process of hiring, incentivizing, and managing a sales force, you're not going to have competent, properly motivated, and well-trained people representing you in the marketplace, and revenues will suffer.

To avoid making too many mistakes and to reduce risk, rapid-growth firms need people who have worked with larger organizations and who know what the firm will look like at a larger scale. These people won't be acting instinctively to solve problems, as entrepreneurs do when making their initial customer promises. Rather, they will be acting on the basis of what they know from experience to be true. They also won't be learning as they go, and thus won't be making the natural mistakes that are part of the learning process. They have already made these mistakes, and they've done so on other people's dimes.

To grow, you need a team with answers, not merely questions. Bringing in outside expertise benefits the firm in a number of tangible ways:

1. **It greatly helps a firm in securing funding.** As we'll see in chapter 5, the hiring of a specific manager can drive a firm's premoney valuation higher by millions of dollars. This is because a competent, experienced management team dramatically reduces a business's risk. To private equity managers, the decision of an experienced manager to come onboard amounts to a powerful endorsement of your venture's potential.

2. **It allows the entrepreneur to concentrate on what he or she does best.** Initially, entrepreneurs are responsible not merely for framing the firm's larger vision but for undertaking all the mundane tasks associated with making that vision come to life. To grow their firms through No Man's Land, entrepreneurs need to shift their roles from doing to designing, from creating to managing others' creativity. With professional managers on staff setting up systems to perform operational tasks more accurately and efficiently, the entrepreneur regains the freedom to help set the course for the company as a whole and to perform the critical task of seeing around the corner.

3. **It sends the message throughout the organization that you're going to be fair.** Remember, people know when a member of the entrepreneur's inner circle isn't performing. When you don't replace a poor performer, it's just not fair.

4. **It brings new DNA into the organization.** Rapid-growth firms need all the fresh ideas and perspectives they can get to help them transition through No Man's Land. The arrival of a new manager amounts to another "high place" from which to view the business. You now are able to look still further ahead, and have more time to adjust to future challenges.

Signs That Original Management May Be Under Strain

- Is your inner circle frozen in its tracks? Are its members looking to you for direction?
- Do all decisions rely on you? Do others in the firm lack authority to make big mistakes?
- Do you feel weary and stretched too thin?
- Do you find yourself making big, process-related decisions based on instinct rather than actual knowledge?

- Do longtime, loyal employees seem in over their heads?
- Is your business asking you questions that you can't answer?
- Do other people in your firm sense that there is a weak link?
- Do you have difficulty finding and retaining new talent?
- Are decisions not being made on a timely basis?

IT'S TOUGH TO LET GO

Management transitions are the most painful issues for leaders of rapid-growth firms to handle. Like other aspects of running a gazelle, management issues are baffling; you know that your current management team is overwhelmed, but you don't know what the precise problem is. Truth be told, you don't want to know. On the one hand, you sense that delegating authority to professional managers could be helpful; you might even look forward, as Glen Davidson did, to off-loading the business to leaders with new energy and ideas. Yet you also know you might have to renegotiate with newcomers which elements need to prevail in the business going forward. You are also reluctant to make changes that would involve replacing loyal staff. In this respect entrepreneurs are rather like parents who dream that their child will win a sports scholarship, yet who know in the back of their minds that this will never happen. They go into denial, ignoring reality to the detriment of all involved.

Can you blame us? Letting go of longtime employees is pure agony. I know—I've had to do it myself. We're talking about firing lifelong friends, the people who followed you into the business when nobody else believed in it. These are the people who dedicated themselves to the cause, who accepted titles instead of pay, who trudged into work when things were so bad that the only strategy was what I call the "Monday Morning Strategy"—come in Monday morning and just pray things work out. The business would not have been born had it not been for their dedication and sacrifice. The fact is, however, that some, or even many, of these people just won't make it to the next level. They don't have the skills the firm needs to move ahead, and, as the entrepreneur, you know it. If you've been waiting too long to make the change, chances are that others in the firm know it, too, but are afraid to say anything.

I was giving a speech some years ago at Virginia Tech. Aside from CEOs, a contingent of MBA students was in the audience, and it was clear from their faces that they didn't have a clue about some of the ideas I was articulating. I was at wit's end trying to describe what the experience of firing or demoting a loyal employee was like, when all of a sudden I had an idea. I called on a young woman in the audience and asked her to think of her best girlfriend in the whole world, the woman whom she calls when she breaks up with her boyfriend, or when she has a fight with her father.

"Her name is Sarah," the student told me.

"Well, I want you to think about Sarah," I said, "and imagine what it would be like to take her to Starbucks, sit her down, and say, 'Sarah, you have been the best friend anyone could have ever hoped for. I couldn't have gotten through school without you. However, now that I am leaving school and moving into the workforce, you really aren't as helpful to me anymore. So I can't be your friend. I'm letting you go. I love you as much as ever, but it's just not working for me.'"

The whole audience sighed, and the poor woman in the audience looked at me in terror, as if to say, "You can't do that. What kind of person would do such a thing?"

I had succeeded in making my point. In my defense, I softened the blow by going on to tell her that everybody wins when the entrepreneur completes a management transition, even, and perhaps especially, the person who has been demoted or let go. Nobody likes to fail, and if the individual in question hasn't been performing up to par, chances are that he or she knows it and feels bad about it on some level.

I'm reminded here of a joke the Mississippi-born comedian Jerry Clower used to tell about raccoon hunting at night with dogs. In the

A View from the Trenches

Judy Starkey, CEO, Chamberlin Edmonds

"I cried when I had to fire one of my most devoted employees. I was up all night the night before. But I had no choice. She was being mean to employees, and she didn't even know it. The worst part was that the next day her husband came to visit her at the office, and he didn't know about it. She hadn't told him, and wouldn't do so for two months. Instead she just pretended she was still employed and sat in the library all day. That was pretty awful. I remember I met her in a mall on a Saturday to do the firing. I drove two hundred miles to get there. Firing has never been easy, but it is invariably the right thing to do, not just for the company but for the person. Once you know you can't make them successful, it's time for them to go. I've never terminated anyone—ever—when it wasn't in their best interests as well."

joke, a hunter has gone up into a tree in search of a raccoon. The raccoon refuses to give in, and quickly starts clawing and gnawing at the man.

"Shoot," the man in the tree says to his friend on the ground.

"What do you mean, shoot?" his friend asks. "I'll hit you."

"Just shoot, damn it. One of us needs relief."

That's the way it is with letting go of a trusted yet unproductive employee. Chances are he needs relief just as much as the firm does, although he might not know it yet.

A View from the Trenches

George Hines, founder, George's Music

"Can you believe it? I almost quit over a management decision I needed to make. I knew we were going to grow, so I determined that I needed to beef up management and bring in an outsider. When I told our general manager, one of our old-time employees, what I was up to, he got real pissed. I thought his emotions would blow over, but they didn't. When the outsider came onboard, the GM worked to undermine him. I didn't know what to do. The situation tormented me to the point where I thought, This is it for me. I'm done. I don't want this stress. I went to Score, the association of retired executives, and said that I was really unhappy and was going to get out of the business. The people at Score said that I needed to sit down with the GM and tell him that if he wouldn't do what I wanted, he had to leave. I followed their advice, and wouldn't you know it, our GM wound up getting a job in another industry."

It's No Fun Being In Over Your Head

Beyond their desire not to cause pain to their trusted employees, entrepreneurs typically shrink from making management changes because they interpret them as inconsistent with the loyalty they feel to their original core group. If someone tells entrepreneurs that they need to let a close friend go, they typically react defensively, acting as if it were somehow their own fault that things have gotten as bad

as they have. They lose confidence in their own decision-making process. Yet entrepreneurs must realize that the transition to outside management is a normal progression; it has nothing to do with entrepreneurs or the particular people they've brought with them on the journey thus far. As a business changes, it requires people with different skill sets. The entrepreneur needs to match the people in charge with the skills the business needs; otherwise the business will fail.

Judy Starkey puts it well: "You hired someone, and at the time this person seemed like a beautiful yacht sailing around the Caribbean. But now you need a huge oil tanker. It doesn't mean that the employee isn't a beautiful yacht—it just means that your needs have changed."

HOW TO HIRE SENIOR MANAGEMENT

The rest of this chapter provides a basic road map for deciding whom and how to hire. Much of what I have to say here is counterintuitive, so rather than lay out my points directly, I'm going to proceed by identifying and destroying certain myths that prevail around the subject of management transitions.

Myth #1: You Need to Determine Where You're Weak, and Hire in Those Areas

This advice isn't terrible; rather, it's the way it's worded that's problematic. Instead of urging entrepreneurs to determine where they're weak, I advise them to figure out their own *strengths*, and then protect them when delegating authority.

Remember the aircraft-parts entrepreneur from the last chapter, the one who knew how to "buy right"? Well, if that's his strength, he doesn't need to hire a hotshot executive from a big company to tell him how to do it. In fact, doing so would probably be a recipe for conflict within the firm—the kind of conflict that Glen Davidson experienced when he hired someone who wanted to do what he did well (i.e., plot the firm's R&D course). Following Davidson's example, what the aircraft-parts entrepreneur needs to do is hire people who can do other things that he *doesn't* do well. He needs to sit down, identify these other areas, and determine which are most in need of immediate attention.

If I were to advise the airplane-parts entrepreneur on what he should let go of, chances are I'd identify "logistics" as something that probably isn't a particular strength of his, yet is critical to the working of his business. If an aircraft-parts reseller is a trading company, it is also very much a logistics business involved with buying, tracking, inventorying, and selling parts. Logistics, of course, involves the same basic elements no matter what industry you're in; it isn't unique to this entrepreneur, nor does it relate to his core business concept. So why not hire someone to take care of it? There are executives out there who have *forgotten* more about logistics as practiced by a $500 million company than this entrepreneur *knew* about logistics as leader of a $70 million company. With ten or fifteen years of experience under their belts, one of these executives would walk in and immediately identify what the business needs—not merely today, but five years from now. His or her decisions would involve much less risk than the entrepreneur's in this area, and the entrepreneur would gain the freedom to focus on systematizing the core value proposition.

Logistics isn't the only competency in which authority can be easily delegated. Often, CFOs are logical people to hire. Developing internal controls, proper costing, and appropriate financial measurements are done across industries in relatively the same way; as such, there's no reason an entrepreneur needs to develop this from scratch. If you as an entrepreneur do try to do it yourself, chances are you won't get it right quickly enough, and you'll wind

A View from the Trenches

Peter J. Chase, president, Purcell Systems

"In our firm, nothing is developed from a product point of view unless you can tie it to a specific customer or group of customers and what they in a fixed period of time are going to buy. Otherwise, nobody is going to buy it. This is something that I'm still keeping my finger on."

up lacking the proper financial information to run the business well. Chaos will ensue, and you'll experience a feeling akin to flying an airplane with instruments that don't reflect the right altitude or wind speed.

I'll say it again: Entrepreneurs need to protect the single most important part of the business, the part where instinctive judgments still come into play. They need to delegate those parts where experience, knowledge, and accurate analytical judgment reign supreme.

Myth #2: To Grow to the Next Level, You Need to Replace Yourself with a CEO

I've heard it said many times that entrepreneurs are not capable of leading large organizations. This is not necessarily true. In some cases, entrepreneurs have exactly the temperament and skills required to bring a company to a billion—and beyond. Just consider what Steve Jobs has accomplished, or FedEx's Fred Smith, or Dr. J. Robert Beyster, the founder of SAIC, the nation's largest employee-owned research and engineering company. Microsoft, Home Depot, Google—I could go on and on, and this doesn't even count the thousands of companies led by entrepreneurs that ultimately grow and get sold to large companies. Conversely, I've witnessed just as many if not more disastrous situations caused by "hired-gun" CEOs as I have those caused by "founder" CEOs. As we'll dramatize in chapter 7, growing the firm into a large, established organization does indeed stand as one of the four possible endgames to No Man's Land, one that entrepreneurs under certain circumstances will accomplish.

One caveat: I do strongly believe that the founder needs to change the organization's gene pool by bringing in other senior leaders to help him. Many entrepreneurs feel defensive about whether they can lead a large company, yet so much of their success actually rides not on them per se but on the people with whom they surround themselves. Moving forward, the founder needs to have people at hand who can make experience-based decisions, not merely the kind of intuitive calls that got the business going and led to the core value proposition's creation.

Myth #3: Credentials Count above All Else in Evaluating New Management Candidates

Of course credentials count; the whole point of hiring is to add people with the experience required to make strong, insightful decisions. Yet it is also important to consider the firm's culture alongside credentials when making a hiring decision, and to communicate cultural expectations to the new hire.

What is culture? First, it is not the same thing as a firm's current products and services; as we have discussed, these will change as customer needs change and as management determines which customers a firm should pursue and grow with. Culture is instead **the set of common understandings that develop around a firm's decision-making process and that support its core value proposition.** Culture is the heartbeat of the organization, the basis for continuity in a time of rapid, wrenching change. One entrepreneur profiled in Bo Burlingham's book *Small Giants* thinks of culture as an "unwritten constitution." "Rome had no written constitution," this entrepreneur says, "just a common understanding about how people should behave. When that fell apart, the Roman empire did, too."[16]

In the case of George's Music, everyone knew that George's decision making on every issue reflected his passionate dedication to musicians, and especially to beginning musicians. In the case of Chamberlin Edmonds, decision making always protected the "soft side" of the business—the requirement that business decisions reflect a genuine compassion for patients—and this is what ensured that the firm treated this constituency with such respect.

When hiring new management, entrepreneurs must balance between continuity and change, between being true to the firm's roots and gearing up for growth, between taking care of the firm's soul and acquiring new capabilities. An entrepreneur's failure to agree with a new hire on what to preserve in a firm's culture virtually guarantees conflict, confusion, and a lasting identity crisis. Chamberlin Edmonds hired a superstar executive with an MBA from the University of Chicago and years of experience at the upper levels of a Fortune 50 firm. As the firm's founder, Judy Starkey, relates, the experience was a disaster on all levels:

> It almost took us to our knees. It was a huge lesson. The fellow we hired came in and it turned out he was an isolationist who kept his door closed all the time, while our culture is much more informal. The guy was also a control freak who didn't want me talking to the employees about their jobs. In effect, he did away with the beating heart of the organization. He created a siege mentality; it was either his way or the highway. Eventually I managed to fire the guy, and the results were striking. While this guy was running things, we had negative cash flow, but soon after we fired him and brought in someone else, we had four million dollars in positive cash flow. It was a total turnaround.

In many cases, the founder herself embodies in her personality the culture of the business. For this reason, an entrepreneur would do well to make sure that she at least likes the person she is hiring, and that the two of them can communicate well. In the end, of course, I can't tell you what kind of personality your management hires should possess. All I can say is that you should temper your assessment of the job applicant's objective credentials with your deepest gut feeling about whom this person really is.

CULTURE CLASH

Below are two fictional letters that illustrate the issues that bedevil the relationship between entrepreneurs and their hired managers.

**From the entrepreneur to the manager hired
into the company:**

September 19, 2006

6243 Fairview Street
Rochester, NY 14618

Pete Stanford
1665 Oak Street
Penfield, NY 16574

Dear Pete:

Now that you've been with us for a few days, I wanted to
write you a quick note to tell you how things stand at my end.
I'm happy to have you on our team. Yet I have to be honest: It's
not all positive feelings here. You don't know this, but when you
came onboard, you entered as a substitute for a family member

I just had to fire. Don't get me wrong: I can't wait to hand off more and more of the load I carry onto you. But you have to understand how much I have riding on this decision to hire you. People around here are traumatized; the guy you've replaced helped build this business, and was loved by his colleagues. On top of it all, I barely know you yet. Deep down, I guess I'm hoping that just having you around will help ease some of the chaos that's running rampant here. I'm hoping for new ideas that I never thought of, yet am scared to death that those ideas are going to be really bad and stupid. Maybe the best thing for you to do is to not have any new ideas for a while, and just focus on getting to know what makes our firm what it is.

After our conversations, I have a funny feeling that your opinion of some of the people in this organization isn't very high. How in the world do I get you to understand not only their weaknesses but also the strengths they've brought to this business? Those strengths are the glue that holds this place together. Sure, there are some things we do differently here, but this is precisely why we've succeeded. And here I am, hiring you because I want to find out how everybody else does it. I hope to heck that injecting some of that collective wisdom into this business doesn't destroy it.

Sincerely yours,

Bud Carlson
Founder, Carlson Interactive Products, Inc.

From the manager hired into the company to the entrepreneur:

September 23, 2006

1665 Oak Street
Penfield, NY 16574

Bud Carlson
Founder, Carlson Interactive Products, Inc.
6243 Fairview Street
Rochester, NY 14618

Dear Bud:

Thanks for your letter. I appreciate the frank exchange of ideas. You know, I'm excited about joining this firm, but I, too, have fears and anxieties. For one thing, I'm beginning to realize that there are a whole bunch of folks who have been with you for a while who are hurt by my hiring. This in turn makes me wonder: Am I going to have a hard time getting them and you to accept my ideas for the business?

You're right about my assessment of certain people in the organization. I can tell right now that there are some folks I don't want on my team, and I haven't even been here a week. Some of these people are part of your inner circle, which makes me even more afraid to let them go.

I know this firm has a strong culture, and that I am not yet a part of it. Yet you hired me to change things, so to some extent the culture has to give. I'm seeing the business do things that don't make sense when you consider where the business is going to be five years from now. To make it worse, a lot of people—even you—are crediting these things with the firm's success to date. I guess I'm wondering if you'll really let me make the changes that, painful or not, need to be made. I hope you'll let me help the company make it to the next level.

Best wishes,
Pete Stanford

An exchange like this is not likely to occur between you and your new manager, but it's helpful—indeed, vital—to be aware of what each of the parties is thinking. I'll analyze the issues that these letters raise in the next section.

Myth #4: Culture Is the Reason Firms Fail to Assimilate Outside Hires

As you can sense in these letters, "culture" often becomes a focal point for the expression of tension between new hires and a firm's existing leadership. When a new hire fails, individual stake-holders often cite culture as a means of avoiding their own share of the responsibility. Why didn't an outsider manage to get anything done? "I couldn't effect change; the firm's culture was too entrenched." Why did the entrepreneur fire the change agent? "He or she was smart, but incompatible with our culture." Why did competent employees quit after a change agent was brought in? "It's no fun working here any-more. The new CEO just doesn't get our culture." Stakeholders need to avoid this dysfunctional way of exploiting culture as an excuse. Un-derstand the culture, respect it, protect it, but don't fall back on it to cover up for your own failings.

New hires need to push for change, but shame on them if they don't show respect for the culture—or, as I've suggested, the decision-making process—that built a successful, growing company. It's a cop-out for a new CEO or new management team to blame culture for an organization's internal resistance; what's really impor-tant is *trust*. Any organization that trusts the decision-making pro-cess used by those new leaders would certainly move to make the changes they advocate. After all, the decision-making process is fun-damentally about *who* is making the decisions. Is this individual trusted to understand what the company can and cannot do? Does he or she listen to those in the organization who really know what is going on? Does the newcomer's decision making reward the right people and get rid of the wrong ones? Does it lead to the right cus-tomer promises and the correct allocation of resources to those promises?

To establish their influence, then, newcomers don't need to over-come culture; they simply need to give those already in the firm a basis for trusting that they will make decisions wisely. And that, in large part, stems from the newcomers' own willingness to show re-spect for founding entrepreneurs. In several of the cases described in this chapter, what was missing from the newcomer's perspective was precisely this respect, as evidenced by the newcomer's marked failure to solicit the entrepreneur's input into critical decisions. Take

PATLive. I happen to know its founder, Glen Davidson, personally, and I can attest that he is a serially successful entrepreneur with an unusual ability to see around the corner. He has succeeded in every endeavor he has initiated. Can you imagine *not* getting him involved in determining the big bets on product R&D? Or take Chamberlin Edmonds: Can you imagine *not* engaging its founder, Judy Starkey, when attempting to develop systems for processes that she developed from scratch?

"Culture" doesn't excuse a newcomer's shortcomings, and it certainly doesn't excuse an entrepreneur's failure to assimilate new talent. Old-timers, including the entrepreneur, need to protect what makes the company special, including the process by which successful decisions have been made, but shame on them for allowing their own egos to prevent newcomers from directly engaging with this process. Isn't it ridiculous to invite a new perspective into a company and then not allow its holder to argue, based on experience, for a course different from that which the original group would have favored?

It all comes down to this: An unsuccessful business deserves a new decision process (or, in other words, a new culture), while a successful growing business needs to preserve the process that made it successful. Since all businesses will prove successful in some areas and unsuccessful in others, entrepreneurs and new outsiders, including successor CEOs, must together cultivate a decision-making environment that incorporates the best of what old-timers and newcomers find important. In other words, entrepreneurs and newcomers must arrive at a mutual understanding about what constitutes the firm's core value proposition, and how decisions concerning it will get made.

There are many ways to arrive at a culture that deftly merges old with new. Rob Wight, cofounder of the software firm Channel Intelligence, was nervous about maintaining his firm's egalitarian, meritocratic, performance-based culture. A former executive at Microsoft, Rob knew that his high-tech, high-performance industry rewarded a firm's ability to recognize and promote talent at lightning speed. He further knew that his firm needed to institutionalize his vision for an organization that judged employees in their assigned roles.

The solution he found was to create a human resources system whereby everyone in the firm is assigned a numerical level rather than a title, where everyone receives a peer-generated performance review and has an opportunity to rate everyone else in the company, and where everyone's compensation is pegged to their performance and their numerical level. "The great thing," Wight observes, "is that everybody's expectations of everyone else are clear. Of course, not everybody can tolerate our culture. So we've lost some good people. But we were recently named the best medium-sized business in Orlando on the basis of our high satisfaction rating among employees. Our system has been core to setting the expectations about how to handle the problem of bringing in leadership."

Myth #5: Professional Management Ensures Profitability and Growth by "Cleaning Up" the Company and Ridding It of Chaos

This myth is especially dangerous. **The real key to growing and making money is to "mess the business up" and "clean it up" in a consistently balanced manner.** As we shall see below, doing so often requires two people, one with an intuitive capacity to "mess up" a business, the other with talents in cleaning the business up. It further requires a mutual respect on the part of each of these individuals for the other's point of view.

If a new hire eliminates all chaos within a firm, something is terribly wrong. A certain amount of chaos within a firm is essential to that firm's well-being, as long as it is balanced by an element of order. As Jerrold Pollack, a neuropsychologist at Seacoast Mental Health Center in Portsmouth, New Hampshire, is quoted as saying,

"It's chasing an illusion to think that any organization—be it a family unit or a corporation—can be completely rid of disorder on any consistent basis."[17] Entrepreneurs need to constantly "mess up" their businesses by making promises to customers that they haven't made before, whether by taking on new customers or serving new needs of existing customers. On the other hand, they need to constantly "clean up" these messes by making sure the firm develops internal processes required to meet the new customer promises. Too much messing up, and the firm dies a fiery death on account of its failure to make good on customer promises. Too much cleaning up, and the firm's customer pool stagnates, causing the firm to die a slow, cancerous death.[18]

Cameron Garrison, founder of the government technology provider Garrison Enterprises, observes that "there's a big pendulum. On the one side is chaos and anarchy, on the other, bureaucracy. You have to keep that pendulum in the middle, but that's tough." Early in their firms' life cycles, entrepreneurs instinctively balance promise making with promise keeping, often without realizing it; because they deal with both operations and marketing, they sense exactly how much they can promise without overextending. As their firms enter No Man's Land, this gets much more complicated. The scales tip too far in one direction; either the firm shrinks from change, or it embraces it too readily, to everyone's frustration. To navigate through No Man's Land, leaders of emerging growth companies must become more mindful of the potentials and obligations inherent in making promises while also taking personal responsibility for maintaining the balancing act.

This can work in a number of ways. In many firms I've dealt with, the entrepreneur retains the prerogative to make the "mess-up" decisions, relying on others for feedback as to whether he's outrunning the firm's capacity to deliver. You can see this in football, too. They used to ask the great Florida State football coach Bobby Bowden why Doc, the team's former trainer, was so invaluable.

Every firm needs a "mess-it-up" person . . .

Bowden's answer wasn't that Doc was the best trainer on the planet, but rather that Doc was the guy he would approach to find out if the players were too tired or down. All entrepreneurs need Bowden's capacity to push the team in new directions, but they also need someone on hand who can play the role of Doc.

Assuming the entrepreneur continues to exercise the "mess it up" function, bringing in an outside executive to "clean up" the business can have a truly profound impact. When Shane Albers started Investors Mortgage Holdings in the mid-1990s, he saw the opportunity to create a great business making short-term, equity-based loans to real estate developers whom banks had turned down. After six years, he had made considerable headway, yet his firm was still a relatively small, local player. Then he brought in Will Meris as a

. . . and a "clean-up" person

partner. Within four years, the private real estate fund they had established had expanded from their home market in Arizona into California and Texas. The fund had a quarter of a billion dollars under management, and was expanding at a rate of $20 million a month.

The key to this success was the balance that now existed internally between "messing up" and "cleaning up." Albers had always been a visionary, especially when it came to putting together and negotiating deals, but he had had little interest in the operational tasks of raising money, hiring and firing employees, and developing the internal systems necessary for his business to scale. Meris, by contrast, was great at those things; before joining forces with Albers, he had built a mortgage brokerage up from nothing to three offices and seventy employees within one year. As Albers reports, "I know where the market can go. I focus a great deal on the vision and on managing the portfolio, and then I'll come to Will and say, 'I need all these people in these areas,' and he'll focus on the execution and the day-to-day running of the business. I'm the gas and Will is the brake. Will raises money and I put it to use in innovative, market-focused ways."

For Albers, bringing in an outsider was not an attempt to eliminate chaos within the firm, but rather, paradoxically, to nurture it. Now that someone is looking after the back end, he is actually freed up to make more and better customer promises. "I'm giving a big chunk of the business over to Will," Albers says, "but I realize that I have to push him into his discomfort zone. In fact, I welcome the chance to do that." Meris concurs, noting that a continued tension between his and Albers's business impulses has been productive, if not always pleasant:

> When we first started working together, Shane's vision made me very uncomfortable. I'd never been around someone who thought as big as him. When we were in a meeting, a potential investor would ask us where we would be in a few years. I'd be saying forty employees, Shane, *four hundred*. Shane still makes me uneasy, which is what I need since I'm used to playing it safe and making sure everything's perfect before moving on. Shane has been the one to give me the kick in the pants, to say that I need to get more done to keep up.

Myth #6: A Growing Company Should Hire in the Middle as a Prelude to Bringing In Senior Management

False, false, false. In fact, the idea that a fast-growth company should hire at the middle is so pervasive and harmful that I'm going to frame the opposing statement as this chapter's navigational rule.

Why hire at the top? Well, to some extent this is a corollary of my arguments above. The point of bringing in outside management in the first place is to have someone with superior experience

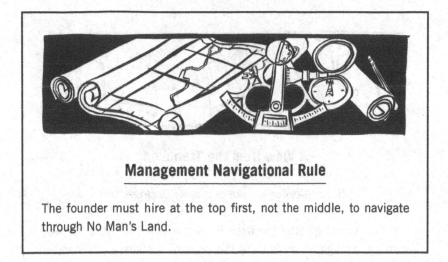

Management Navigational Rule

The founder must hire at the top first, not the middle, to navigate through No Man's Land.

who already knows what the various endgames look like and what it takes to get there. Only a senior-level hire will have the ability to make the experience-based decisions the firm needs. Look at it this way: You don't build a house without hiring a seasoned architect or contractor as part of your team. If you rely on a contractor who is learning on your house or on an architect fresh out of grad school, the house will most likely be flawed, or else it will be built inefficiently. In construction as in business, you need to find someone who can organize solutions *ahead* of problems, based on experience, not someone merely able to keep pace with the problems at hand.

Hiring at the middle also increases rather than eases the burden on the entrepreneur. I can't tell you how many times I've seen a founder strung out and desperate for help, only to find that his or her mid-level hire lacks the necessary experience and is constantly turning back to him for direction. Remember, you're looking to hire an expert who can "own" a chunk of what is now—or will soon be—a process-laden business. You're looking to delegate authority, not extend your own authority over yet another employee who is hamstrung and in over his head.

A View from the Trenches

Bruce Moeller, president and CEO, DriveCam

"When I hire, I go after the best of the best. Not everybody agrees with me, though. I had to force the issue of overhiring at the top— the board just didn't see it. I literally had one of the board members say to me, 'Look, just because Donald Trump might be available doesn't mean you have to get Donald Trump.' I said that it sure does. Not that I want Donald Trump per se, but in my view the business deserves nothing but the best, and I will accept nothing less. They looked at me as if I was crazy and a spendthrift."

MANAGEMENT *M* PAUSE POINT

This chapter has examined how critical it is that founders of emerging growth companies get managers onboard with the skills required to take the firm to the next level. Now, you're probably thinking: "Hey, Doug, I'd love to transition from instinctive decision making to experience-based decision making. But how am I going to afford it?" As we'll see in chapter 5, it's gotten harder in recent years to afford top talent thanks to the compliance requirements of Sarbanes-Oxley. On the other hand, given the capital markets' tendency to reward businesses that can attract seasoned executive talent, it will be costlier *not* to take the plunge and hire experienced managers who command respect.

Beyond possessing the right management team, an emerging growth firm needs to convince the capital markets that it has a clear economic model for making a profit as the firm scales. We'll examine the issues surrounding economic models in the next chapter. For now, please sit back and think through the management issues we've examined here. Keep in mind that failure to complete the management transition means that you will never get out of No Man's Land. So if you just can't bear the thought of firing the people who need to be fired, if you can't fathom letting others handle big parts of the business, or if you aren't willing to take the financial risks that hiring top talent entails, then stop, because traversing No Man's Land is not for you. You will find so much more fulfillment staying small, or selling out to someone else who can take the firm to the next level.

Management Pause Point Questionnaire

Fair warning: The questions that follow are going to make you a bit uncomfortable. As we will discuss in chapter 6, most entrepreneurs have an inner circle that they rely on when making decisions. Yet that inner circle is going to need to be shaken up. Whom to let go is not a decision that requires a lot of consultation with others. In fact, I'll bet that right now there is tightness in the pit of your stomach because you already know the person or persons who have to be dealt with.

1. For each member of senior management, outline the single thing they most excel at in your opinion.

2. What do you believe you individually are best at managing in your company?

3. Put down on a piece of paper the process that you use to make the most important decisions in the company, and include the names of people whose opinion you seek, if any. Only include the names of people who have changed your mind in the past—the ones in your inner circle.

4. Provide one example of a decision made by a member of your management team that you believe was a mistake based on a lack of experience. Outline consequences to the company of that mistake.

5. How many members of your senior management team have had experience in a senior management position with a company that had at least five times your current revenue?

6. If you could manage only one part of your business, which would it be and why?

There is one other issue that needs to be addressed. Many of you have made an implied promise to your original core group of followers in good faith. It sounds like this: "When we get there, trust me, I am going to take care of you." The problem is that each of those who have received this promise adjusts what "taking care of them" means over time. The gap between what you believe is appropriate and what some of your core team believes is appropriate can be shockingly vast. In a number of situations I have served as the new CFO in an organization where I immediately began a process to ferret out and document those expectations. Trust me, now is better than later. So here is the question:

7. In your business, are there some unresolved promises to "take care of someone"?

I told you this stuff wouldn't be easy, so let's end with a dramatic story that illustrates how making the tough calls can lead to a happy ending. In 1976, Doug Groves went to work for Carapace LLC, a distributor of building materials run by his father and uncle. The firm sold Formica laminate, wall paneling, moldings, flooring, and other products, bringing in about $2 million in annual revenues. By 1980, Groves had become familiar with the business and its customers, and was growing excited about an opportunity to distribute what he saw as a promising new product, DuPont's Corian surface.

Unfortunately, the firm's general manager, a longtime employee, was not a risk taker and was reluctant to invest in Corian. Groves pushed the issue, arguing that the firm should invest money in Corian and in cultivating a relationship with DuPont. Groves prevailed; with the backing of his father and with his business partner, Carapace made a number of investments in Corian during the early 1980s, including the buyout of a Baltimore-based Corian distributorship. Yet the general manager continued to oppose these decisions, and tension in the firm mounted.

By 1985, Carapace brought in a consultant to resolve the conflict. After painful deliberation, the general manager was taken out of the picture. And here's the happy ending: Freed up to follow his vision, Groves nurtured Carapace's Corian business, driving revenues higher and higher. Today Carapace distributes Corian throughout the southern United States and enjoys a strong relationship with DuPont. Although revenues from the product are leveling out, Corian and related materials still bring in more than *$80 million annually* for Carapace. As Groves reports, "Our tremendous growth only occurred once the GM was out of the picture. Making the tough management decision really was the key to a whole new chapter in our business's history. It's helped make us the firm we are today."

Tackle your management problems, and you, too, could unleash your firm's true potential.

4

Outgrowing Your Model

Most entrepreneurs attract their first customers by running their businesses according to a "high-performance, cheap labor" economic model. By the sweat of their brow, and with the aid of dedicated employees, they provide superior products and services at below-market cost. As a firm scales upward, however, this economic model breaks down, and the firm must begin to pay market wages and adjust to a normalized cost structure for its products or services. To make it through No Man's Land, firms must develop a new economic model that allows them to provide its value proposition at scale and earn a profit. In addition, the firm must constantly analyze its performance in light of this model to assure that the company will achieve sustained profitability.

SHOW ME THE MONEY

As a law student during the early 1990s, Tom Lynch taught himself computer programming, and found that he loved it even more than he did the law. Although he wasn't willing to drop out of law school, he decided to complement his studies by getting a part-time job writing an inventory system for a computer store. After graduating, he passed the bar and was immediately engaged to try his first court-room case. His client won, but was awarded only one dollar in damages. Lynch couldn't believe it. The next day, he founded a software development company. He had had enough of law and its hollow victories.

For Lynch, starting his own business proved to be exactly the right move. On the basis of its superior client service, his firm, Infinity Software Development, became one of the fastest-growing businesses in America, ranking number 486 on the 2002 *Inc.* 500, with five-year revenue growth of 459 percent. By 2005, the firm had $20 million in revenues and 173 employees, with an additional staff of about 30 contractors. Not bad for a company in a commodity business facing competition from large multinationals such as Accenture.

Today Lynch has proven that he can make money as a local player selling to private industry and the Florida state government out of offices in Tallahassee. Yet he finds himself in a difficult situation. Given the competitive nature of his industry, Lynch fears that his business will not be able to compete indefinitely at present scale. To retain his main resource, top-quality talent, he needs to offer attractive career advancement opportunities, which in turn means winning larger, more challenging assignments in additional locales. Winning these assignments would also help Infinity to build its brand, which would in turn create whole new levels of opportunity.

Lynch plans to open several new offices out of state. He thinks that he will be able to replicate his firm's culture of customer service and make a profit at larger scale, but he is not sure. He is inclined to take the plunge, since the risks of *not* growing might be even greater. Yet he's nervous. "The decision of whether to grow is really tough," Lynch says. "I've got a good thing going now, but it just isn't sustainable. On the other hand, who knows whether we'll make money at a larger size. I've got some people on the ground in other states right now, and I'm looking for the right opportunity. But I have no idea what the future will hold. I guess you could say I'm in No Man's Land—*big time*."

Lynch's predicament is hardly unique. As businesses grow, entrepreneurs typically find themselves confronting huge changes in their business models. In Lynch's case these changes are arising as a result of a strategic decision to expand, but more often entrepreneurs put a strain on their models without realizing it, experiencing as a result a general sense of economic malaise that they don't understand. Beyond feeling overworked and out of sync with customers, these entrepreneurs feel as if they don't know where the business is *financially*. They don't know whether they are making or losing money, or whether growth is improving the business or running it deeper and deeper into the ground. On a day-to-day basis, they feel like their business is operating on fumes, and they don't know where their next infusion of cash will come from. Finally, they feel a sense of heightened risk, as if every decision they make entails betting their personal financial future, or the firm's very existence.

Where the business model is concerned, No Man's Land is a scary place to be. So what do you do about it? I'll provide some ideas later in the chapter, but first let's step back and take a brief—and I mean brief—foray into everyone's favorite topic, accounting. Before entrepreneurs can secure their firm's financial health in No Man's Land, they need to understand what a company's business model is, what a change in that model means, and what rapid growth does to unsettle a firm's financial performance.

SNEAKING A PEEK AT THE FUTURE

When I speak of a business model, or, as some call it, an economic model, I mean something quite specific: an analysis, *in financial terms*, of how a business makes money. Looking at an economic model means considering the capital deployed, the revenue produced by selling products or services to customers, and the changes in these elements of revenue, cost, and capital under different scenarios.

Accounting has two main tools at its disposal to analyze firms financially. On the one hand, it takes a *still photo* of a business's assets and liabilities at the end of each month. This still photo is called the balance sheet; it describes the firm's assets and reveals how those assets came into the business, either as liabilities or as owner's equity (capital provided by owners and earnings retained in the business). In fact, all of accounting is based on one simple equation: **Assets = Liabilities + Owner's Equity**.

What accounting also does, though, is compare this still photo with another still photo taken a month earlier, arriving at a video of how the firm's photo—i.e., the balance sheet—is changing over time. This video is called the income statement. The income statement provides a notion of the new assets that have come into the business ("revenue") and the assets that have left the business ("expenses").*

Balance Sheet "Snapshot"

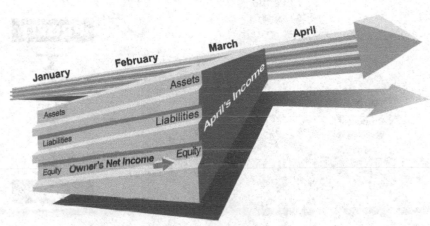

---

*Note that the concept of the video extends to include not only the income statement but the cash-flow statement and the statement of changes in owner's equity. The illustration is simplified to include the income statement alone.

Neither balance sheets nor income statements give rise to a firm's economic model. This is because both of these tools are *backward-looking;* they convey information about the firm and how it has performed in the past. An economic model, by contrast, is *forward-looking.* It projects out to the future, speculating on what a firm's economic picture will look like based on a likely scenario. In keeping with our entertainment metaphor, we can say that the business model allows entrepreneurs to preview the movie of their businesses before they start the process of actually living out the movie. An exercise that entails forecasting a company's business model is important for two reasons: first, it helps entrepreneurs decide if they actually want to commit to the contemplated strategy under consideration; and second, it gives the company's leadership some basis for evaluating how a business is actually performing (i.e., against the projected model) once it embarks on the journey.

In order to predict what the future photo of your business might

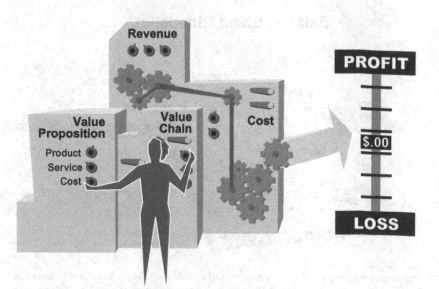

look like, you have to understand the photo's (i.e., business model's) primary parts—revenue, costs, and capital requirements—and how those parts interact. Let's take a short moment to perform an exercise that will illustrate the concept of thinking about your business in terms of an economic model. We will start with a scenario that likely takes place every day in your business.

Estimate for me how many net employees you have added to your business in the last twelve months, and how much you have ended up paying them, fully loaded with benefits, on an annual basis. A rough estimate will do, one that includes only those employees who represent overhead. If you are a consulting firm, don't include the revenue-generating/client-facing employees; if you are in the construction business, subcontractors don't count.

Write them down:

# of net new employees _____
Average fully loaded annual compensation _____

Now let's get started. Joe is a supervisor in some part of your growing business and he approaches you, asking for a meeting. You inquire about what you should expect at the meeting, and Joe says that he needs to sit down with you and discuss getting the folks in his department some help. "We have too much work for the number of people I have," he says.

The meeting takes place the next day. You ask, "Joe, what do you think you need?"

"I need at least five more people based on the work that I hear is coming down the pike."

"Well, what about transferring work over to Bob's area? Wouldn't that solve some of the problem? With our benefits package, the entry-level employees going into your department cost a minimum of fifty-six thousand dollars per year."

Joe frowns. "Hey, but look at the overtime we are incurring now. There is just no way we can keep up. I'll tell you what—let me go with three rather than five, and we'll figure it out." You agree, thinking that another problem related to accommodating your growth is behind you.

Sound familiar? Now let's turn this conversation around to get you thinking in microeconomic terms, or, in other words, in terms of a business model. The meeting starts exactly the same way, with you asking Joe what he needs. He responds, "I need nine hundred thousand dollars to automate a large piece of our process based on the work that I hear is coming down the pike. In fact, what I want to do will help out Bob in his area."

"Are you crazy!!!" you respond. "You're asking this business to invest almost a million dollars—I can't afford to do that."

Now take a look at the schedule below:

CAPITAL COST OF EMPLOYEE

7 year, 8 percent term note

Borrowed Equivalent	Salary Monthly	Amount Annually
100,000	1,559	18,703
150,000	2,338	28,055
200,000	3,117	37,407
250,000	3,897	46,759
300,000	**4,676**	**56,110**
350,000	5,455	65,462

This schedule lays out the capital cost equivalency of a single employee making approximately $56,000 per year. The economic equivalent of hiring one person can be compared to borrowing $300,000 at 7 percent, amortized (i.e., paid back) over seven years. In other words, paying a salary on $56,110 requires the same amount of resources as borrowing and repaying $300,000. What this means is that **hiring three people is the economic equivalent, on a cash basis, of borrowing $900,000.**

I imagine that many of you are saying, "I couldn't borrow $900,000 for my business if my life depended on it." But if you could borrow the money, you would probably try to determine whether these funds, if invested in the automation, would actually pay off in the future. Running through your mind would be the thought that if you borrowed that kind of money, you would have to live every day with the pressure of paying it back. Further, you would have to survive a loan officer's skeptical review of the risk that it will not be paid back.

Psychologically, it's far easier to hire the employees. There is no loan officer whose approval you need, and besides, if you get into real trouble you can always let the employees go. My point here, though, is that the consequences of adding three people are really quite significant when viewed in economic terms. If you were employing financial capital rather than human capital, you would instinctively attempt to look into the future so as to determine how that money would be deployed. You would think through scenarios, determining whether the risk of not getting a significant enough return would outweigh the benefits of putting that money to work. Consider, by contrast, how quickly you make critical decisions in your business every day—such as how many people to hire—without assessing the compound consequences they have on the company. Such assessment is precisely the kind of analysis that I am going to ask you to employ on your entire business by the end of this chapter.

THE HIGH-PERFORMANCE, CHEAP LABOR MODEL

During the start-up phase, most entrepreneurs don't construct formal models for their businesses. Rather, they understand the financial interrelationships of their businesses *intuitively*. They know whether they're making money or not by the end of the month even before they get historical financial statements. Since they involve themselves intimately with both marketing and operations, they understand how their revenue relates to costs, and how costs relate to the promises they make to customers. To the extent that they use historical financial statements, they use them to confirm, not create, their understanding about how the business's operating components perform financially.

Yet most early-stage emerging growth firms can in fact be analyzed in terms of a common economic model, what I call "high-performance, cheap labor." Early on, firms are profitable because they pay below-market wages to offer superior products and services. Most of the core leadership could make more money working for someone else, yet they consistently deliver extraordinary performance. The entrepreneur serves as the chief source of the firm's value proposition, thus allowing for high-touch, attentive customer service. The combination of high quality and low cost is often what allows start-ups to snag their initial customers and create momentum for early growth. Indeed, the high-performance, low-cost business model is both simple and powerful. It is business at its most efficient and streamlined, business pared down to its essence.

In the case of Infinity Software Development, Lynch and a core group of early employees built the business by working insane hours and taking home cut-rate wages for years. Lynch contributed his own expertise not merely in software programming but in listening to clients and determining what they really needed out of a project. Drawing upon his prior, pre–law school experience working at IBM, he developed a unique client interaction method that involved identifying the stakeholders, getting them in a room, building a business plan for the project, and creating a glossary of specialized terms. Over time, the process became increasingly sophisticated, making use of a designated facilitator and a protocol of exercises and techniques. This became the firm's unique value proposition and has led to a brand that has allowed Infinity Software to compete with and beat large competitors in the industry.

And remember George's Music from chapter 2? In the beginning, the business was all George, all the time. In setting up the business, George found a five-thousand-square-foot store for rent and renovated the entire thing himself. Since he didn't have nearly enough inventory for a five-thousand-square-foot store, he built a wall and kept moving it back as the inventory expanded. For two and a half months before the store opened, he booked music lessons himself. Once the store opened, he spent long hours clerking behind the register. His own personal guitar collection helped serve as the store's initial inventory stock. This labor was high-performance in that George did everything possible to ensure the store's success ("I was on a mission from God," he says). It was also dirt-cheap. During those early years, George put all profits back into the business, and survived by living a student's lifestyle and staying at a girlfriend's apartment.

Today, of course, George has dozens of employees handling operations in his ten stores. Likewise, Lynch no longer writes code himself or participates directly in project delivery—he stopped back in 1997. This points to a basic observation about high-performance, cheap labor as an economic model: It is unsustainable with growth.

As a business expands, it will eventually grow beyond the individual entrepreneur's capacity. At this point, a new reality rears its ugly head: The firm must normalize its cost structure, continue to deliver value, and, ultimately, deliver a profit.

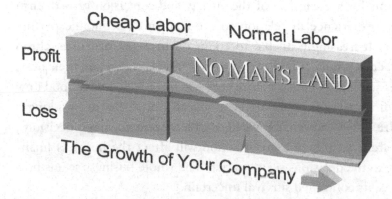

The limits of high-performance, cheap labor

All of us want to have people around the organization who are as passionate as we are. Ultimately, though, you can't build an organization on superhuman effort. Sustainable profits must be built on normal people doing normal things for normal compensation. Goldman Sachs has the smartest people in the world working their hearts out seven days a week, but the people in the company make an average of five hundred thousand dollars a year—and as a writer for *The Economist* observed, that includes a lot of secretaries. The whole business, in other words, is built on outrageous performance, which in turn is reflected in outrageous compensation.

It is possible, of course, to evolve a high-performance, cheap labor model into a very profitable small business built around the entrepreneur and leveraging his or her unique talents. A perfect example is a friend of mine who had very significant experience as an industry consultant, and who was able to acquire several large customers as a result. Leveraging his expertise with that of consultants who worked for him, he made upward of $1 million a year and paid his staff normal market wages. Yet he didn't scale the business upward to the point where it took on a life of its own apart from him. Rather, he achieved a stable small business by organizing it around his own personal talents and efforts.

The gradual erosion of high-performance, cheap labor typically accounts for a great deal of the anxiety and confusion growth-firm leaders experience in relation to the company's economic performance. Increasingly unable to count on high-performance, cheap labor, entrepreneurs find their profit margins eroded and their businesses stalling. Whereas before they had intuitively understood how their firms were functioning economically, now they are no longer so sure. They experience vertigo; called upon to make decisions, they aren't sure how a given action will affect the business financially, so the decisions seem scarier. The whole business seems precarious, its continued survival uncertain.

Markers of a High-Performance, Cheap Labor Economic Model

- Entrepreneur is the chief source of firm's value proposition
- High-quality goods, services delivered inexpensively
- Relies on below-market labor of a committed core group
- Unsustainable with growth

IS YOUR VALUE PROPOSITION SCALABLE?

Firms in No Man's Land struggle when their previous models for making money break down, leaving them without a clear understanding of financial processes. To get out of No Man's Land, firms have two options: They can either return to a size where their models work well, or they can attempt to grow their way out of No Man's Land. To proceed down this second path, firms must develop an understanding of how their current business model will change as it moves from high-performance, cheap labor into scale.

The essence of what must be determined and calculated is captured in the following navigational rule:

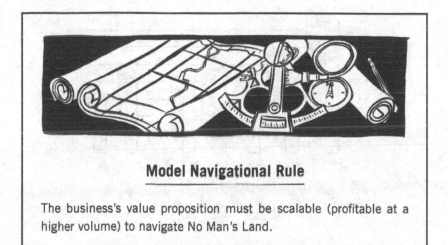

Model Navigational Rule

The business's value proposition must be scalable (profitable at a higher volume) to navigate No Man's Land.

Applying this navigational rule is a multistep process. First, entrepreneurs must determine whether they can contemplate a profitable economic model for their business at a higher scale. This is by no means a trivial matter; some businesses will be profitable only as small operations framed around the entrepreneur. On the other hand, there are businesses that will survive only if they *do* scale. Infinity Software Development is one such example. Another is First Standard Freight, a company we encountered in chapter 1. In the latter case, consolidation in the logistics industry has created a situation where only behemoth firms and specialty, niche firms can compete profitably. Midsized firms such as First Standard are being squeezed out. Sorting through his future scenarios, First Standard's founder, Rick Shelley, needs to determine if a future profit zone would exist for his business at its present size of about $20 million in revenues. Otherwise his best option will probably be to sell out to a much larger competitor.

Shelley reports having felt intuitively that market forces were

Analysis of the Freight Forwarding Market, 2000–2005
Pre-Tax Profit Percentage by Five-Year Average Firm Size

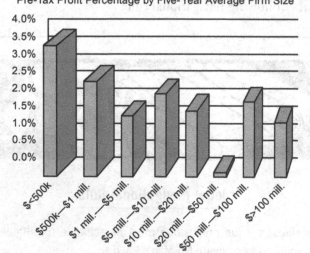

Source: Data provided by Advanced Data Technology, Inc.

squeezing him. Selling, in his view, has come to seem like a much safer bet. As it turns out, Shelley's instincts reflect some amazing marketplace patterns. Consider the data for his industry in the graph on the previous page—no profit between $20 million and $50 million.

As part of a scalability analysis, industry information proves critical; competitive marketplace pressures play a key role in determining what a firm has to do to navigate successfully into a profit zone. As the chart above shows, profitability in Shelley's industry has in fact become clustered around companies both larger and smaller than his own. To survive, he may need to become part of a much larger firm.

Shelley's situation illustrates the kind of high place you need to get to as you evaluate whether your business can execute the navigational rule. Determining a business's scalability requires intuitive judgment about the future—what Peter Drucker refers to as "the entrepreneurial skill." But it also requires an economic analysis of how your company's model will likely change as it approaches scale. You need to step back and become radically objective, using every tool available to assess your business and glimpse the future before you move into it.

Industry dynamics is hardly the only thing that growth-firm leaders need to consider when assessing their models' future scalability. Take, for instance, a firm I encountered while serving on a panel gathered to help companies prepare for a Red Herring conference. As some of you know, local Red Herring conferences are put together to expose promising emerging growth companies to private equity investors. The firm here was founded by technologists out of Georgia Tech; its software product had already attracted a number of Fortune 200 customers and was generating revenue and profits. In making their presentation, the firm's founders explained that they needed money for a sales force if they were going to scale up.

"What kind of sales force are you going to implement?" I asked.

"Uh, well, a sales force."

"Do you mean the kind of sales force that gets on an airplane, visits prospects, builds up relationships, rebuilds relationships when the decision maker changes, et cetera?"

"Well, yeah."

"So how long is the typical sales cycle?"

"Four to six months."

"And how much do you sell your product for?"

"Thirty-five thousand dollars."

"I hate to break it to you," I said, "but you'll never make it. You can't support a direct sales structure with a product that only sells for thirty-five thousand dollars."

This company was operating in the high-performance, cheap labor mode. The company's president was not only its chief designer but also its chief salesperson. With an innovative product that had attracted the interest of big companies, company leadership figured, "Why not just go out and take on a few million dollars in private equity, add a sales force, and grow the company?"

Yet I had reviewed economic models that analyzed the normalized cost structures of emerging growth software companies. I knew that in order to support the cost structure of a direct sales force, a software company had to have a product that sold for many multiples of thirty-five thousand dollars. Selling directly to the Fortune 1000 usually demands a lengthy sales cycle, so to make a profit, the product's price must be sufficiently high. No doubt the firm here would have experienced increased sales, but it would have never reached a profit zone.

As it turned out, several of the other panel members, including the CEO of a publicly traded software firm, agreed with me and even elaborated on my observations. We saved this firm's leadership some embarrassment: Had these guys sought private equity, prospective investors would have come to the same conclusions as we did.

When designing their business models, so many firms fail to consider just how expensive it is to identify and acquire new customers. Distribution channels—the mechanism used by a firm to identify and acquire a new customer—are by far the most expensive components of the business model, costing even more than delivering the value proposition. The software company in this example hadn't figured out how they would acquire customers without the founder's high-performance, cheap labor. For them, it was back to the drawing board. They would never obtain capital unless they could create a less expensive mechanism for acquiring new customers. Failing that, they would have to sell to another, larger company that already had a Fortune 1000 sales channel and could profit by adding its product to their product arsenal.

More generally, firms testing their business models for growth need to consider not merely the source of their revenue streams but the expenditures required to support those revenues. Some costs remain the same independent of revenue, whereas others increase as revenue does. Each of George's Music's retail stores incurs the same rental costs, utilities, insurance, etc., regardless of the amount of revenue. On the other hand, certain costs develop as a firm no longer relies on high-performance, cheap labor and grows into a business that is sustainable apart from the contributions of the founder and the core group. As we saw in the case of First Standard Freight, Inc., for instance, market forces driven by regulatory changes made it necessary to invest in a sophisticated Web capacity that tied the business with its customers electronically.

Such costs make sense when we remember what a firm is actually doing as it expands. As we saw in chapters 2 and 3, growing firms must develop processes, systems, and professional management to deliver customer value at scale. If the business is going to grow beyond the entrepreneur's personal capacities, the business must become good at what the entrepreneur was doing, and this costs money. In the case of Tom Lynch's Infinity Software Development, opening new offices means investing in an infrastructure that includes not only more real estate but the human resource systems required to replicate the firm's culture of superior customer service across the network of offices. As Lynch reports, "We already know how to handle health plans, paychecks, et cetera, in the back end. We have documented processes in place, especially as relates to employee growth. But expanding those systems costs money. If we're going to go for growth, we're putting everything on the line. But for what?"

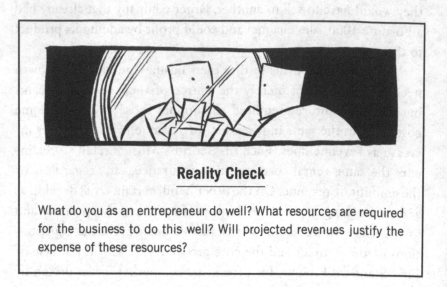

Reality Check

What do you as an entrepreneur do well? What resources are required for the business to do this well? Will projected revenues justify the expense of these resources?

THE CASE OF DRIVECAM

Sometimes developing a viable business model for expansion can cause considerable turmoil within a firm. As an illustration, consider the case of one exciting young company, DriveCam.

DriveCam started when a young Australian entrepreneur with a technical background had a brick thrown through his car window. He was so infuriated that the weekend after, he invented a camera device that could be mounted inside a motor vehicle to monitor driving events. The device had cameras pointed both inside and outside the vehicle, and it was programmed to save only those portions of video imagery taken immediately before and after an unusual driving event.

The entrepreneur had a product; now he was tasked with finding a market. In January 1998, the company went into business selling the camera system to consumers as a means for them to monitor their children's driving behavior. The firm attracted start-up capital, and managed to attract some customers, yet results were modest. By 2004, after a period of turmoil brought about by 9/11, the business had stabilized into a small but profitable concern, with about $2 million to $3 million in revenues and just under twenty employees.

That year, the company was looking for a new CEO, and a board member happened to think of Bruce Moeller, an experienced corporate manager who was also a behavior modification specialist. Moeller visited the firm and immediately realized that the firm was leaving incredible amounts of money on the table. Rather than marketing the camera as a product, the firm would have an astonishing amount of potential if it instead used the camera to market behavior modification services under a recurring revenue model. The real target customer, Moeller realized, wasn't consumers who would buy the product once and then have no further dealings with the company, but rather businesses with large fleets of vehicles. These businesses would partner with DriveCam on an ongoing basis to reduce risky driving among employees and thus save 30 to 90 percent on their insurance and workmen's compensation costs.

Rather than a $2 million to $3 million business, Moeller saw the potential for DriveCam to become a $1 billion business. The board agreed, and decided to bring him on to implement the new model. Scarcely had he arrived, though, than he realized that the board, in fact, was split between those who were willing to put money behind his vision of a new model and others who saw no reason to risk what was already a small yet profitable venture.

Moeller got an early boost when he visited one of DriveCam's best customers, the school bus company Laidlaw. He discovered that they had instituted a safety course based on Moeller's own principles of behavior modification. They had already been using DriveCam as a behavior modification device, though the company itself didn't know it. "From then on," Moeller recounts, "it became a question of how to institutionalize this within DriveCam—how to turn it from a product company to a service company."

Moeller went on to develop a recurring revenue model whereby DriveCam installed and monitored the devices in the fleet vehicles of client companies, analyzed the data, and created reports on an ongoing basis. The response from investors was highly positive. Large private equity firms came in, engaging in a bidding war on the basis of the new model. Moeller wound up raising $18 million in capital when he had initially planned for only a few million. Certain members of the board, however, remained unconvinced, especially when it became apparent that some of this money would be used to hire the professional management necessary to implement the model. "I had to force the issue of overhiring at the top," Moeller recounts. "Certain members of the board just didn't see it. I needed the capital to lower the risk to the executives I needed to grow this company, not just to fund the company's growth."

With the infusion of private equity, Moeller finally had the resources to drive conservatives off the board. Making highly attractive offers to certain angel investors, Moeller was able to consolidate power and steer the company in the direction he desired.

So far, it's paid off. By 2006, the firm had installed DriveCam devices in forty thousand fleet vehicles, with clients that included taxi companies, bus services, and other transport firms. The firm had ninety-seven employees, and was adding five to ten employees a month. Revenue was also expanding dramatically, from $15 million in 2005 to a projected $28 million to $30 million in 2006.

As Moeller will be the first to admit, getting DriveCam to change its model midstream was difficult. Now, though, with a solid model, the right management, and sufficient financing in place, the firm is poised for stratospheric growth. Its best days, Moeller thinks, are ahead of it.

NEGOTIATING THE OBSTACLE OF STEP-FIXED COSTS

The DriveCam case illustrates the importance of developing a viable model for profitable future growth. Yet it isn't enough for entrepreneurs simply to determine if their firms will be profitable at a higher scale. They must also establish precisely *when* their firms will become profitable.

As the figure below illustrates, the costs a firm incurs as it expands do not always correspond exactly to revenue flow. Rather, those costs occur in what I call a "step-fixed" transition. A firm must invest money in infrastructure *in advance* of revenue, building a pipe big enough to handle anticipated *future* demand volume. It is essential, then, that entrepreneurs know how big they need to grow in or-

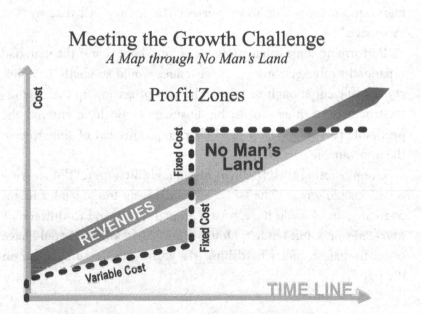

Meeting the Growth Challenge
A Map through No Man's Land

der to pay for the investment. Otherwise, they risk investing money only to arrive at a place where their businesses cannot turn a profit. If firms don't expand enough to put their revenues into the next profitable section of the graph, they risk wasting away where they already are: in the unprofitable section.

For a cautionary tale, consider the predicament of a subway sandwich shop franchisee who approached me after a presentation I made about No Man's Land. "Doug," he said, "I'm in No Man's Land. I had three subway shop stores, and I was making a ton of money, so I decided to expand. But now I've got eight and I'm barely breaking even."

I asked the man why the business was profitable at three stores, and he told me that his costs had been relatively low, since he had done much of the work himself. When an employee called in sick, he filled in. He performed the hiring and firing himself and also went around personally to collect cash from each of the stores and deliver it to the bank. With eight stores, however, his personal efforts no longer sufficed. "I've had to create a whole new infrastructure," he said. "I've had to create a human resources department, and a controller who oversees the money. All that stuff is expensive."

Performing some calculations, we figured out that if the man had expanded to thirteen stores, his revenues would suddenly have become sufficient enough to justify the cost of setting up the new infrastructure. In other words, his business would have entered the profitable part of the step-fixed cost graph, instead of lingering in the unprofitable part.

Upon learning this, the man became visibly upset. "I'm so frustrated I could scream," he said. "You see, I went to the bank and got financing, and I could have gotten enough to expand to thirteen or fourteen stores, but I didn't. Doug, if only I had known. I could have saved myself so much hardship. My entire business might be on the line."

STAYING ON TOP OF THE CURVE

Okay, you've laid out a viable economic model for growth, and have figured out how large you have to grow in order to become profitable again. What else do you need to do to make it through No Man's Land?

Two things. First, you have to monitor your firm's financials to make sure your firm is performing according to the model. This is where the income statement, the balance sheet, and other operational statements come in. While such backward-looking accounting tools are not adequate to guide firms through the financial dimensions of No Man's Land, they are invaluable as compasses that allow you to figure out where your firm is at any given time relative to the model.

When I served as copresident of Archibald Enterprises, I was running an incredibly complex corporation that at the time comprised Homes and Lands Publishing, the largest franchised real estate publisher in the United States; Vista-Chrome, one of the largest graphics and prepress companies; and The Printing House, one of the largest printing operations in the Southeast. Our operations spanned more than three hundred locations, including several large production facilities, each with hundreds of employees. As I soon discovered, however, the key driver for the whole business was whether there was work stacked up in front of the presses and the presses were continually running.

Prepress is all the work you have to do to put a plate on a press and run a bunch of copies. We realized that if the presses were constantly running, we were printing money. If the presses were waiting for the prepress work to be completed, the business was in trouble.

In those days, prepress processes were labor intensive. As a manufacturing genius, Del Archibald had designed a series of processes that dramatically expanded prepress capacity, reducing prepress time. The cost advantage we received through the company's unique prepress innovations allowed us to print color less expensively than anyone in the world. This huge cost advantage for short press runs became both our value proposition and our underlying, sustainable, and scalable competitive advantage. Understanding prepress bandwidth and the larger effects of prepress operations gave us a huge handle on the company's economic model. It was very simple: We had to make sure the presses were always running. The extent to which they were constituted a valuable performance measure, which is why we always received daily and weekly reports on our prepress operations.

Operational reports are critical as instruments that let you know where you are in your path to growth. When a firm is in No Man's Land, it is rapidly transitioning from one economic model to another, and as a result it is not enough merely to have a big-picture understanding of the financial performance. You need minute-by-minute feedback. Having it gives you back the sense of control you lost when the high-performance, cheap labor model started to break down. Effective measurements allow you to reestablish through systems and data inputs the financial calculations you used to do in your head when the firm was smaller.

Reality Check

Do I have a series of operational reports that let me guess with accuracy at the end of the month what my net income is?

The final thing entrepreneurs need to do to make it through No Man's Land, once a viable model is in place and the next profit zone is on the map, is simply to steel themselves and hang on for the ride. Financially, traversing No Man's Land is nothing less than a forced march through dangerous terrain. Your firm might lose money in the transition, particularly if your business requires a dramatic step-fixed cost increase in infrastructure, but you have to keep at it, having faith that your economic model will ultimately drive you into the next profit zone as you grow. And this points to one of the most important benefits of creating future scenarios based on your firm's business model: Thanks to the thinking work you've done, you now have the confidence to move ahead and keep

When Transitioning to a New Model,
You Ultimately Need to Hang On

the momentum going, even if the company is losing money in the short term.

To bolster your spirits, I end this chapter with a story of how extreme faith in a model can pay off. During the mid-1990s, Cameron Garrison developed a radio show in which he announced egregious restaurant health-code violations on file at the local Department of Health. The show was a great hit, prompting Garrison to realize that the public had a tremendous, unsatisfied hunger (pardon the pun) for this kind of information. In 1999, Garrison started a newsletter and accompanying Web site, which printed health-inspection reports verbatim for three cities in North Carolina. Although he soon had thirty thousand subscribers in Charlotte alone, he wasn't happy. He was finding that his business was both capital-intensive and labor-intensive, and that he wouldn't be able to scale without securing $20 million to $30 million in investment capital. In addition, he realized that the coming digitization of government records would give citizens ready access to Health Department material, thus rendering his services obsolete.

In 2001, Garrison had an epiphany: If government would soon digitize its records, maybe he could have a piece of that action, at least where health departments were concerned. He went back to the Health Department in Charlotte and presented the in-house software his firm had developed to keep track of the health-inspection reports they had pulled. Would the Health Department have any interest in purchasing a modified version of such software? Their jaws hit the floor. So Garrison drove out to Los Angeles and New Mexico to see if the health departments out there would respond similarly. They did, and a business was born. There was one catch. Before he could sign any deals, Garrison would not only have to revamp his software to turn it into a viable product, he would also have to completely dismantle his publishing business, since government clients would never hire him if they thought he was merely trying to publish their information.

By this time, Garrison Enterprises had revenues of a couple of million dollars. Convinced that he now had a model that was scalable over the long term, Garrison decided to jump in and immediately transition his firm from a publishing model to a software model. Money was scarce; for six months, while the new software designers Garrison had hired were fine-tuning the product and Garrison was landing his first customers, the firm had zero revenue. To save money, Garrison was forced to downsize. "This was wrenching," Garrison remembers. "I had to let twelve people go in one day, for no fault of their own." Equally wrenching was the task of pushing the business forward without the prospect of immediate revenues. "I had to shoot a perfectly good business in the head just to start another. To this day, I have no idea how we did it. I had all my credit cards maxed. I had to drive everywhere, and I put two hundred fifty thousand miles on my car in one year. It was craziness!"

Yet Garrison persevered. In March 2002, he landed his first client, and a couple of months later he had a revenue stream flowing from his new product. "We were building the product as we sold it," Garrison recalls. "I would call in from the field and say, 'We need these four features, because the client asked for it and I agreed.' We created a product that captured the market's pulse."

By 2006, the business had grown and stabilized, with six hundred customers across the country and revenues of $3 million. "It's harder to be nimble now," Garrison says. "We're steering a business with thirty people and we have so much coordination to do, so many customers to satisfy." Looking back on the six-month transition, Garrison remembers the uncertainty as the hardest thing to deal with. "The worst was when I walked into a customer's office and they said, 'We love what you're doing, but we're going to wait a year and see how you're doing then.' Nobody wanted to be the first one in—and I didn't know if we were going to make it." But the firm did make it, something that to this day prompts wonder on Garrison's part. "These days, I don't think I have the guts to shut down a business and start another. I've lost some of my risk-taking, shoot-from-the-hip style. But hell, I did it. Garrison Enterprises is living proof—something like a model change can be done."

MODEL *M* PAUSE POINT

The issues surrounding a firm's economic model raise the question once again as to whether you as a growth-firm leader should continue to grow your business. Is your firm viable at greater and greater scale, or do you risk growing yourself out of business? Are the fruits of growth worth taking the risk of making infrastructure investments up front? Once again, it's important to step out of day-to-day operations and get to a higher place. Think about your firm in grander terms: As a machine for making money and creating value, how does it work right now? How might it work going forward? If you can't come up with a model that allows for profit at a greater scale, then growth really isn't for you. Maybe your destiny is to lead a small, stable, and highly profitable firm based on your own unique talents. If so, there's no shame in that.

Model Pause Point Questionnaire

Instead of a series of questions, I present a single one designed to help you regain financial control. As we've seen in this chapter, assessing how well the firm is living up to its model involves determining the primary operational drivers that predict revenue, cost, and profits. With this in mind, pose the following question to your financial staff:

1. What kind of operational report can you create that will allow me to predict, with an accuracy of within +/−10 percent, the company's net income, prior to creation of the end-of-month financial statements?

Your financial and operations folks will need time to address this challenge. Most gazelles already lack bandwidth in financial functions; you're asking them to delve down to the essence of what drives the firm's performance and to get you the data accurately and in a timely fashion. Give your staff the time it needs by affirming that this project is a higher priority than creation of the financial statements by the tenth of the following month. Make a contest of it; tell your staff that you will buy them lunch every month that they allow you to guess the company's net income within 10 percent by the last day of the month.

You can't run your firm by looking backward to see what already happened. For this reason, the monthly financial statements you receive should merely confirm your preexisting understanding that the firm is operating according to its model. It will take a few iterations for your financial team to get it right, but creation of a viable operational report represents the only way for you to regain financial control and retain confidence in your business model.

As we've seen in this chapter, growth is a tricky proposition. Firms need to invest capital in front of revenue to create high-octane, high-volume infrastructure. But where does this capital come from? How do firms find the economic resources they need to deliver themselves out of No Man's Land? This brings us to the subject of the next chapter, the fourth *M*, money.

5

Outgrowing Your Money

Most companies enter No Man's Land without enough capital to leave it. If and when they fail, "undercapitalization" is seen as the cause. Yet undercapitalization is not the cause but rather a fatal symptom. The true cause is a company's inability to raise capital because it is perceived as too risky. To raise money, firms must focus on reducing their real and perceived risk by addressing the issues described in the previous three chapters. Yet even with the appropriate measures in place, transition through No Man's Land is difficult because of institutional barriers that exist in the capital markets. Hang on—it's going to be a wild ride.

DON'T MESS WITH MONEY

In 1998, Assurance Medical, Inc., a Dallas-based company that outsourced drug-testing services, was on the fast-growth track with clients such as Frito-Lay and Southwest Airlines. Yet the firm faced a challenge. If it was going to take on AT&T and several other large companies as new clients, it needed to ramp up its telephone service center, hire more employees, and make a number of other structural changes. And that required up-front cash, to the tune of $2 million to $3 million.

The firm's founder, Harden Wiedemann, was optimistic. He approached early-stage investors and venture capitalists, eager to tell them about his promising business and to offer them a piece of the action. Surprisingly, everyone declined. The problem was not Wiedemann's business, but the amount of money he needed—$2 million to $3 million. This was too much for early-stage investors and incubators, but not enough for the venture capitalists.

As the months dragged on, the strain on the business and on Wiedemann himself grew greater and greater. "We really beat the bushes," Wiedemann says. "For a full year, that was pretty much all I was spending my time on. The problem is that looking for capital takes you away from the operational aspects of the business. Customer service is the reason we got those companies, and that started to slide when I couldn't keep my eye on the ball."

Frustrated at every turn, Wiedemann decided to switch directions and transform Assurance Medical into a Web-based application service provider, rather than an outsourcing partner. "We actually had a commitment from a venture capital group," he says. "If the migration had panned out, we would merge with two other companies and get five million dollars. Then the e-commerce market started to erode, and the venture capital company pulled out."

In January 2001, Wiedemann was forced to sell Assurance Medical to First Hospital Corporation, based in Norfolk, Virginia. The transaction cost twenty employees their jobs, but, more than that, Assurance Medical lost the opportunity to hire more workers and continue growing. "We could have been as big as fifty to one hundred employees and twenty million dollars in sales if we had been able to get interim financing," Wiedemann says. Wiedemann shakes his head. "It wasn't that the company went out of business. The problem was that we had *too much* business to service with the resources we had. We had more contracts and demands for services than we could fund out of cash flow."

Capital shortfalls are one of the most frustrating and terrifying issues that face firms in No Man's Land. Shortfalls frequently emerge just as the firm is gearing up to grow through No Man's Land, leaving entrepreneurs in the position of poker players who hold unbeatable hands, yet no longer have any chips to bet. But we're not talking about a poker game here. Lack of capital is scary because it can bring a once healthy firm to its knees—and with it, the entrepreneur. Entrepreneurs in Wiedemann's position have little choice but to sell or retreat from growth, because at this point in the business, financial failure means sustaining *personal* losses, even bankruptcy.

MISCONCEPTIONS ABOUT CASH FLOW

Why do rapid-growth companies run into money troubles? A big problem, unfortunately, is confusion about financing. Leaders of rapid-growth firms generally underestimate the capital that their firms will require to emerge from No Man's Land. They fail to secure the necessary financing, and as a result their firms run out of fuel just as entrepreneurs are beginning to solve the other growth-pain issues discussed in this book.

What most entrepreneurs fail to realize is that growth itself generates the need for capital. As we saw in the previous chapter, the phenomenon of step-fixed costs means that a growing business requires capital *in advance* of revenue. Yet the financial dimensions of growth are trickier than that. Even when a business is and remains profitable, growth requires infusions of capital, for the very reason that it *eats up cash flow.*

Now, hold on. Did I just say that right? Is it possible to turn a profit and still have a cash-flow problem?

Look around, and you'll find many rapid-growth firms out there that are rolling in profits, yet have no cash on hand. Worse yet, they have more cash going out than coming in. As one expert on emerging growth businesses has remarked: "It is perhaps counterintuitive that success, the very thing we applaud in all young companies, should lead to an early and critical need for cash that some businesses simply cannot overcome, but it is true."[19]

In the simplest context, consider a wine-importing business that purchases $100,000 worth of merchandise from vineyards in France. The business pays up front in cash, places that merchandise in inventory, and ships it to a retail customer in the United States. The customer in turn agrees to pay in sixty days. During the interim period, the wine importer will reflect a gross profit in its financials on the shipment, yet show a negative cash flow of $100,000. Now imagine that we're talking about $200,000 in wine; in this case, the firm now has a $200,000 cash shortfall. You see the problem: The faster the firm's orders accelerate, the more profit it makes, yet the lower the cash flows.[20]

A few years back, I met with senior economists at the Federal Reserve to discuss the microeconomics of firms in No Man's Land, and even they didn't understand that you could be making money yet still have more money going out than coming in. I'll never forget what it was like, sitting outside the room where they set the nation's interest rates, and poring over t-accounts, one of the most basic tools of accounting, with these distinguished economists in an effort to help them understand.

On this occasion, and during testimony before the House Small Business Committee, I used a series of schedules to dramatize growth firms' very real cash-flow predicament. Here they are:

Microeconomics of Growth

The typical asset growth characteristic of a rapidly expanding business transitioning through No Man's Land using the accrual accounting methods

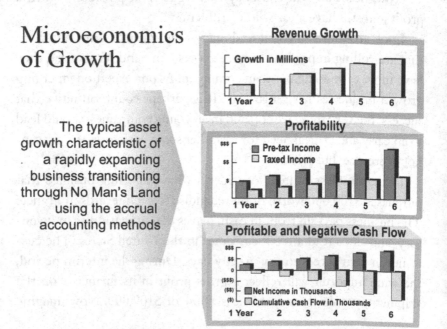

As these charts suggest, businesses that reach a certain threshold grow faster and become more profitable, but also require more cash. Think of it this way: "Net income" on accrual-based financial statements predicts cash flow by approximating how much cash your business will *eventually* generate. If your business wasn't growing and it made a million bucks during the year, all things being equal, your business at the end of the year would show an additional million dollars in cash. Yet if you take most businesses up the growth curve rapidly, the million dollars shows up in inventory, receivables, or even infrastructure—in other words, in noncash assets. The cash will catch up on the balance sheet only when the business slows down.*

My aim here is not to make you chastise yourself for failing at company-level microeconomics, but rather to alert you to a critical problem facing your business. As a result of the speed of change, the leadership of gazelles often loses its ability to predict their business's cash needs far enough in advance to provide for the company's finances. To take up the driving metaphor again, entrepreneurs don't know how to read their fuel gauge, and as a result they all too frequently find themselves running on empty. Then they grow desperate. They make bad decisions about customers, investors, and partners. Sensing the size of the opportunity before them, and the consequences of the potential failure, they sometimes lose their integrity. This, truly, is a moment of maximum vulnerability.

AN EVEN BIGGER PROBLEM: THE CAPITAL GAP

In the case of Assurance Medical, though, misconceptions about money weren't really the problem. Harmon Wiedemann knew he

---

*I recognize that for you accountants out there, this is an oversimplification, but I think it makes the point.

needed capital, and he even knew how much he needed. What he didn't know was where to get it.

He's not alone. Floyd Kvamme, cochair of the President's Council of Advisors for Science and Technology, has remarked that "[t]he number one priority of emerging growth companies is, and always has been, sufficient and efficient access to capital."[21]

To fund start-ups, many entrepreneurs rely on their personal credit to obtain funds. They mortgage their homes, borrow money from friends and family, and rack up debt on their credit cards. At a certain point, the business needs more capital than the entrepreneur personally can repay. Lenders must then make credit decisions on the basis of the business's merit rather than on the entrepreneur's personal credit score. Unfortunately, the economic models of most banks and private equity firms make it very difficult to provide capital to these firms, since the costs of performing due diligence and other administrative tasks on the capital provided become prohibitive.

As economists and policy makers are beginning to realize, America's rapid-growth firms are currently at a distinct disadvantage when it comes to raising capital. In a letter sent to a senior administrator at the Treasury Department, I presented the results of interviews my firm did with senior management of several regulated and nonregulated financial institutions. As a nonregulated asset-based lender told us, processing a loan entailed costs in three areas: loan acquisition (allocated cost of a seasoned loan officer or originator), asset monitoring (borrowing and reporting frequency workload), and the risk-adjusted cost of capital to the lender. Based on their analysis of these costs, the lender determined that they could not profitably provide capital to a business with asset-based lending needs below $1 million at a rate of less than 25 percent. This constraint was confirmed in an interview we did with the senior executive of a super regional community bank holding company. A major commercial bank we interviewed revealed that their minimum loan threshold for assigning a credit officer was $5 million.

There's plenty of seed capital around to fund start-up ventures in this country, and plenty of private equity to fund established firms that have transitioned through No Man's Land and have capital needs of $5 million, $10 million, or more. Yet there's a range of capital need—say, between $250,000 and $5 million—that the capital markets simply aren't servicing.* In fact, macroeconomic data from the Small Business Administration report *Small Business Lending in the United States* confirms that there is a quite dramatic drop-off in the number of loans between $250,000 and $1 million (see table below).

NUMBER AND DOLLAR AMOUNT OF SMALL BUSINESS BANK LOANS, JUNE 2000

Loan Size ($)	Dollars (millions)	Numbers (millions)	Average Loan ($)
Under 100 k	121.4	9.80	$ 13.4 k
100 k–249 k	88.0	0.73	120.5 k
250 k–1 million	203.5	0.63	361.1 k
Totals, Small Business	412.9	11.16	495.0 k

As analysis of this chart reveals, loans to businesses of between $250,000 and $1 million represented only 5.6 percent of the 11.16 million outstanding small business loans by banks in June 2000. Furthermore, it would appear that a significant portion of the loans in this category were close to the bottom of this range where personal assets might be involved as the principal form of loan security (e.g., one bank interviewed used personal credit criteria for all small business loans up to $500,000). The SBA report indicates that "since [the

---

*Experts vary in their assessments of this range's exact limits. Dr. David Sampson, assistant secretary of Commerce for Economic Development, puts the problem area at between $50,000 and $2 million. As he reports, "Funding at this level tends to fall between the cracks of existing capital markets." David A. Sampson, assistant secretary of Economic Development, Department of Commerce, "Entrepreneurship in a Growing Economy," Federal Reserve Bank of Kansas City, fourth annual Rural Policy Conference, April 28, 2003.

value] of large loans (over $1 million) are increasing most rapidly, the concern still exists that small firms may not be obtaining the credit they need to grow with the economy."[22]

Capital Funding Gap
Capital Funding Source and Risk for Emerging Businesses

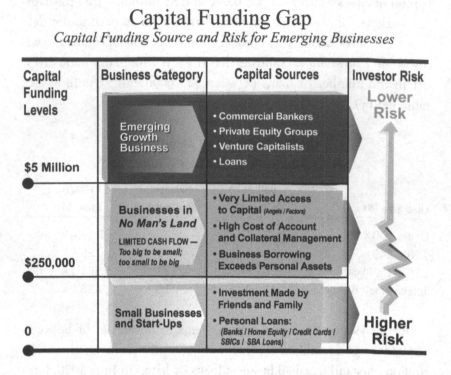

Capital Funding Levels	Business Category	Capital Sources	Investor Risk
$5 Million	Emerging Growth Business	• Commercial Bankers • Private Equity Groups • Venture Capitalists • Loans	Lower Risk
$250,000	Businesses in No Man's Land LIMITED CASH FLOW — Too big to be small; too small to be big	• Very Limited Access to Capital (Angels / Factors) • High Cost of Account and Collateral Management • Business Borrowing Exceeds Personal Assets	
0	Small Businesses and Start-Ups	• Investment Made by Friends and Family • Personal Loans: (Banks / Home Equity / Credit Cards / SBICs / SBA Loans)	Higher Risk

As a result of the capital gap, entrepreneurs like Wiedemann are flat out of luck, irrespective of their firms' potential. And this is a shame, for both individual entrepreneurs and the economy as a whole. The costs are huge. Every year, some of our country's most innovative and exciting firms are needlessly thwarted for lack of capital. The following two case histories illustrate the extent and nature of the problem.

THE CASE OF DOCUSOURCE

If capitalization weren't an issue, Les Walker, CEO of DocuSource, would have built his sales organization and aggressively sought sales throughout Southern California, not just in Los Angeles and Orange counties. "We would have placed sales branches in new marketplaces, signed more customers, hired more service and field technicians, and even added administrative support," Walker explained in 2001. Instead, DocuSource trimmed its staff from more than one hundred to only seventy employees, kept its focus largely on L.A. and Orange counties—and was even considering the sale of the company. "We were in a vise where there was a tremendous market opportunity, but we weren't in a position from a capital standpoint," Walker said. "Instead of increasing revenue and employment, we were reducing our workforce so we could work within the realities."

DocuSource should have been on top of the world. The innovative office-equipment company, which provided integrated software- and hardware-based document management solutions to businesses, grew 700 percent over an eight- to nine-year period, to more than one hundred employees and $21 million in sales in 2001. It ranked 159 in 1995 on *Inc.* magazine's annual list of the nation's five hundred fastest-growing companies. The *Los Angeles Business Journal* counted DocuSource among the fastest-growing private companies in Los Angeles for six consecutive years. Although clients were primarily from Southern California, its national accounts included the prestigious CB Richard Ellis. "We were a good example of an emerging growth company that had the ability to compete and provide alternative solutions to the largest players in our industry," Walker says. "Our challenge was capitalization in order to sustain our level of growth."

So what was the problem? As Walker reported, the company's current bank was increasingly cutting back on the firm's borrowing power, while efforts to negotiate a line of credit from a replacement bank were unsuccessful. "We were in a cash stranglehold with the current lender," Walker says. "Banks tightened up their underwriting criteria." DocuSource was equally unsuccessful in its efforts to raise $1 million in subordinated debt. "We offered a 20 percent annual interest rate, and at this point had only raised about 40 percent of what we need, with half of that total coming from the owners."

Incorporated in 1990, the company first ran into trouble in 1998, when it expanded its product line and its marketplace. From a one-product company in the Los Angeles County marketplace, it began to offer three product lines in a territory that included seven Southern California counties. The catalyst was Ricoh Corporation's development of the first digital copier, which it sold through authorized dealers such as DocuSource. DocuSource seized the opportunity to sell the latest and best technology to a broad range of customers. The drawback: "It took a tremendous amount of investment to bring it on. We had to train the sales staff, train or hire field service technicians, and expend capital to inventory the equipment, parts, and supplies. There's no question," Walker says. "If we had additional capital, we would have built our sales organization and become aggressive with the other Southern California counties; we would be placing sales branches in those marketplaces."

Instead, DocuSource was reluctantly considering the sale of the company, which would undoubtedly lead to further layoffs. "The acquiring company probably does not need all our infrastructure—which means that the economy would be better off with us as an independent company than if we're acquired and duplicate personnel are laid off."

THE CASE OF ELLIOT WEINMAN

Weinman, a Massachusetts entrepreneur, started two fast-growth companies over a twelve-year period, ramped them up to several million dollars in revenue—then was forced to sell both of them when capital needs outstripped cash flow.

Weinman established the first company, Software Productivity Group, in 1989, working from his home. "We produced magazines, ran conferences, and performed analyst consulting services," he says. "Our clients were large companies that were buying enterprise software and software-development tools." In 1990, the company's revenues totaled about $100,000. By 1993, the total had grown to $2 million, and by 1995, $3.8 million. By the time the company was sold in March 1996, it numbered about twenty-five employees.

"It all sounds great," Weinman concedes. "The problem is that when you're growing, you've got to pay your payables. You can't push them more than sixty days." And Software Productivity Group's payables—primarily for printing and postage—were substantial. By contrast, cash receipts from accounts receivables were taking three to six months to come in.

By the end of 1995, Software Productivity Group had grown to twenty-five employees, had moved into a new office in June 1995, and was generating almost $4 million in revenue. "We were on track to do almost $6 million in 1996." But it wasn't to be. "I needed to increase magazine circulation at a cost of over $400,000, expand and move the office again, and hire more people. The tax bill was going to be more than $300,000, and we needed working capital of at least $200,000. Since January and February are typically slow months in our business, we also had to fund about $150,000 in overhead through March 1996. Although I had set up a $100,000 revolving line of credit, I couldn't successfully grow my company on what was left," Weinman says.

At that point, Software Productivity Group was approached by a privately held roll-up company called Ullo International. "Ullo was prepared to cash us out and invest $1 million in the company," says Weinman, who accepted the deal, albeit reluctantly. "If we had been better capitalized, I would have kept the business."

Weinman founded another company in late 1997, Intermedia

Group, a high-tech conference and consulting business. This time he accepted $300,000 in venture financing from META Group, a publicly held company (NASDAQ: METG). Once again, the company grew rapidly. It did $450,000 in revenue in 1998, $1.9 million in 1999, and $6.2 million in 2000. "We were a nice-sized company, doing business across the country. We had about $1.3 million in cash by the end of 2000."

However, this was barely enough to fund the fast-growing company's needs. Intermedia paid $750,000 in taxes and $300,000 in expenses during the slow months of December through February. It also had to begin funding the marketing expenses for the March and April conferences. With no conferences planned early in the year, income was minimal during the first quarter. Weinman was left with about $250,000 in the once hefty bank account. Again, with cash needs of at least $250,000 to $500,000, Intermedia Group was a target for a takeover. "When you are growing quickly in the $1 million to $10 million range, you start to compete with larger companies very quickly. Our competitors on the low end were $30 million to $40 million conference companies. On the high end, we were also competing with large, traditional information technology publishing companies whose annual revenue was greater than $1 billion."

Instead of continuing to grow as an undercapitalized business, Weinman accepted an offer from Internet.com (now INT Media Group, Inc.—NASDAQ: INTM) to buy Intermedia. "I believe it's better for a small company to grow big and succeed than to get sold," Weinman says. "I would rather have a business. I think most entrepreneurs would."

SO WHAT SHOULD I DO?

Sorry, but in this instance a certain amount of doom and gloom is inevitable. There is no magic bullet for entrepreneurs struggling to navigate the capital gap. In the last chapter, I'll discuss a couple of things government could do to ease the plight of rapid-growth firms. Failing that, though, many entrepreneurs are essentially left in crisis mode, trying to find capital as best they can, trying to engineer a miracle.

There are some steps entrepreneurs can take to at least maximize their chances of surviving the financial perils of No Man's Land. The first is creative crisis management. Faced with an imminent

A View from the Trenches

Peter J. Chase, president, Purcell Systems

"The capital markets opened up to us when we did about $21 million in revenue. We had $9 million in financing come in that time—this was spent to take us international and bring in the right people. Before we got capital backing, however, there were some rough times. On one occasion payroll was coming up, and there was no way I was going to make it. I called a friend of mine, told him I needed $15,000. He said, 'Done.' On another occasion, we got really lucky. Facing obligations we couldn't meet, we woke up one day and found out that $80,000 was wired to us. We weren't sure why. It turned out to be an early payment from one of our customers. The company said, 'Oh, we just want to establish good credit with our valuable vendors.' Man, that money came just in time. Of course, the customer in question soon went out of business. It's a tough world out there."

cash shortfall, entrepreneurs can resort to all kinds of improvised, patchwork approaches to fill in the gaps. Some entrepreneurs, like George from George's Music, negotiate creative, low-cash leases with landlords. Others turn to friends or family members for short-term loans to handle specific obligations, such as payroll or utility bills. Burt Prater, the entrepreneur we met in the introduction, went to his leasing company and said, "We can't pay you for four or five months, but after that we'll start paying rent again and we'll add twenty percent." The leasing company wasn't happy about it, but they had little choice other than to agree.

In addition to paring back cash expenditures as much as possible, companies can and should take steps to assure their earliest possible access to capital. So critical are these steps to the firm's future well-being that I encapsulate them in the following navigational rule:

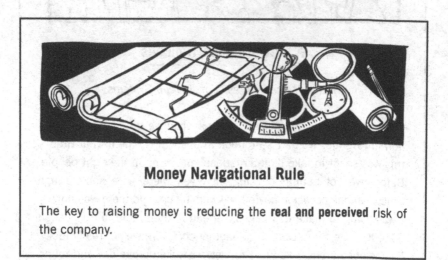

Money Navigational Rule

The key to raising money is reducing the **real and perceived** risk of the company.

Entrepreneurs have to navigate the capital gap and actively prepare themselves for the capital markets. Unfortunately, many entrepreneurs assume that lenders and private equity firms are most impressed by the size and scope of their business's future earning prospects. In fact, lenders and, to a great degree, private equity investors approach the funding decision from an entirely different angle. They do care about upside; but what they're really interested in knowing about is *how risky* a business is. Remember, most traditional lenders don't participate in the upside. What they really want to understand is how they are going to get their money back. Private equity firms approach the business in much the same way, protecting their downside with liquidation preferences negotiated on the equity they purchase.*

While a company may have tremendous upside potential, then, to maximize its chances of raising money, it needs to reduce its real and perceived risk. In other words, it must prove that it can indeed escape No Man's Land.

How does a business do this? Simple: by taking real steps related to the previous three *Ms*. Once the firm is realigned with its market,

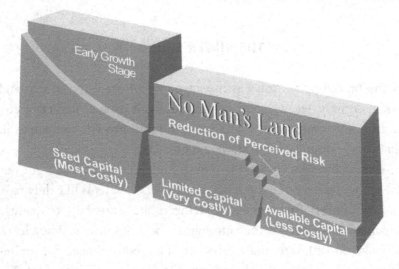

---

*When I use the term "private equity," I refer to a group of investors who manage others' money specifically for the purpose of investing in private companies. Private equity comprises both venture capital firms that tend to specialize in early-state ideas, usually in the technology or biotechnology fields, and what have been traditionally referred to as buyout firms. Buyout firms or leverage buyout firms are generally the investors we find in the gazelle world. Remember, less that 10 percent of gazelles are high-tech. We will discuss private equity and the issue of liquidation preferences that are used in a typical private equity deal in subsequent chapters.

once management issues are dealt with, and once the firm develops a model for scaling profitably, the real and perceived risk goes way down and the company stands a far greater chance of accessing the capital it needs to continue to grow.

Most entrepreneurs view money as the problem rather than as a symptom of other problems. "If I just had money," they say, "I could get to the other side of this difficult terrain." Yet money is not the most basic challenge facing the entrepreneur—all these other things are. Sure, money is essential to the success of a rapid-growth firm, but it is not a magic bullet. You have to deal with the other three *M*s and bring the business's operations onto solid ground in order to *get* the money. To the extent that you view money as the problem, you are actually diverting yourself from dealing with the other three *M*s. You are missing the *real* problem.

THE SILVER LINING

If the preceding section has not managed to erase the gloom and doom entirely, let me point out that difficult capital markets aren't all bad. They can actually be a boon to rapid-growth companies in that they encourage innovation and efficiency.

Remember MacGyver, the eighties television hero who got out of scrapes by jerry-rigging tools out of everyday items like duct tape and lightbulbs? Entrepreneurs facing capital shortfalls frequently become MacGyvers in the running of their businesses. They learn to make do with less, and it pays off. The reduced need for capital increases the odds in the short term that they'll make it through No Man's Land, while the resulting efficiencies can continue to benefit the firm economically even after the capital markets have opened up.

And then there is the fact that many businesses *do* manage to make it through No Man's Land. Once they do, they are poised to take advantage of this country's wide-open capital market. As I've seen time and again, the capital markets open up precisely at the

Reality Check

Can you think of long-term positive attributes of your business whose innovation was prompted by cash-flow issues?

moment a firm passes out of No Man's Land. It makes sense—when a firm is out of No Man's Land, it is more stable and the risks are lower, making it far more attractive to lenders and to private equity firms interested in funding its further growth. And can you imagine what it feels like to have investors knocking on *your* door for a change? It's incredible. You've made it through adolescence, and you've survived. On a financial level, and in fact in every way, you have so much less to worry about.

In some cases, companies that have repeatedly been denied capital wind up making it through No Man's Land with help from unforeseen sources. Consider the dramatic example of Snapper. In the early 1960s, a lawn mower was developed in Georgia that promised to revolutionize the way lawns were mowed. At that time, mowers were mostly push machines with blades that spun like the huge harvesting combines. This new machine, by contrast, used a rotary blade that spun horizontally under an iron protective shell, driven by a small gas engine. It looked a lot like a turtle. The company that made it was called the Snappin' Turtle Mowing Machine Company.

Sales of the Snappin' Turtle mowers were growing at a turtle's pace until an entrepreneur named Bill Smith bought the company and started making changes. First, he reduced the weight of the shell by changing the material from iron to steel. Next, he shortened the name to "Snapper." Third, he hired a salesman named Tony Malizia, giving him part ownership in the company. Tony put a mower in the back of his station wagon and set about recruiting dealers, mostly hardware stores, to carry the Snapper mowers. Other technological innovations were developed for the Snapper mowers, including a vacuum system for the cut grass and leaves and a patented "bag between the handles" bagging attachment.

By 1968, with sales approaching $10 million, Bill and Tony saw a great future for Snapper mowers, but they did not think they could get the financing to realize their vision. To achieve the economics of manufacturing, they would have to produce the mowers almost year-round, even though retail sales would be concentrated in the spring and early summer. Furthermore, to achieve their desired growth rate of more than 20 percent a year, they needed to spend money on plant and equipment to produce ahead of demand. They also needed financing for inventories of materials, parts, and finished mowers, and they would need to provide seasonal financing for their dealers to take the mowers in advance of the retail buying season.

They approached banks, but to no avail. Turning to private investors, they couldn't entice the major players to invest in such a small deal. Smaller players were interested, yet they judged the prospects so risky that they wanted to exact an excessive price for their participation. Finally the two men met J. B. Fuqua, an entrepreneur who understood and embraced their vision. Through his public company, Fuqua Industries, Inc. (then NYSE: FQA), Fuqua agreed to fund the growth and let Bill and Tony continue to operate their company without interference. Snapper was sold to Fuqua Industries, and the growth story really began.

With tremendous grass-roots (pun intended) advertising by their dealer network and support from the distributors, the Snapper brand became well established in the 1970s. Sales grew. And grew.

Profits, meanwhile, were unusually high due in part to the year-round manufacturing, and in part to the high quality of Snapper's products. In the 1970s and 1980s, Snapper consistently delivered a 20 percent pre-tax operating margin (profits as a percentage of sales) while growing between 20 and 25 percent in sales per year.

By 1988, Snapper had grown to $300 million in sales and had financed its growth through high profitability. During the previous twenty years, Snapper had also sent to Fuqua Industries more than $100 million of surplus cash in dividends. Not content with the high vacuum deck and the "bag between the handles" in walk-behind mowers, Snapper had developed a rear-engine riding mower that had the advantages of better forward visibility and no exhaust in the face for the owner. The Snapper rear-engine rider became a status symbol among suburbanites, signaling their determination to own only the very best.

Just because financing is difficult to come by doesn't mean companies don't get it. If the capital markets reject you, then apply the four *M*s, make do with less, and keep the faith. It's all you can do, and it just might be enough.

MONEY *M* PAUSE POINT:
THE CHALLENGES OF CAPITAL

No discussion of money would be complete without considering one of the most pressing sets of challenges a firm has to deal with as it passes out of No Man's Land: managing the relationship with investors.

As anyone who's been through No Man's Land knows, taking on capital is as much an art as a science. Lenders and vendors are not intimately involved in a company's future; they don't have an investor's stake. Yet an outside equity holder does. When entrepreneurs finally sign the big private equity deal, they are forging a relationship they've never encountered before. This relationship is not similar to an employee relationship, nor does it bear much resemblance to the bonds with customers. Rather, it's more like adopting a new son- or daughter-in-law into the family. All of a sudden, you have to set a new seat at the table, and you have to learn to deal with a whole set of new and unfamiliar social interactions.

An underlying source of tension is the radically different perspectives investors and entrepreneurs bring to the table. Investors look at businesses abstractly, from what we've been calling "a high place." Entrepreneurs, meanwhile, have been in the trenches. They have no empathy for anything other than the company that they've started and built up from scratch. Investors see capital as a means to improve the condition of a business that is already fundamentally healthy. For entrepreneurs, capital frequently appears as a magic bullet, a solution for all that ails the firm.

Tensions in the relationship boil over when unforeseen complications arise. In the beginning, investors sign on to a company and its formal business plan. Yet all of a sudden, new circumstances force the entrepreneur to make adjustments. This puts the entrepreneur in a difficult position: He feels an obligation to adhere to the original plan, yet also wants to respond and react as his instincts are telling him. Meanwhile, the investor is concerned. "I know problems arise," she thinks to herself, "but you, the entrepreneur, need to be perfectly up-front and transparent about what is going on." The entrepreneur wonders: "Oh, boy, this is going to take more capital than I thought. What are they going to think of me when I ask for more?" The investor, meanwhile, always has more capital allocated for each of its investments, assuming the rationale for an additional infusion of funds is sound.

When the entrepreneur-investor relationship breaks down, the primary culprit is typically a failure in communication. To circumvent this situation, I'd like to conclude this chapter by offering two fictional letters, one written to the investor from the entrepreneur, the other to the entrepreneur from the investor. Taken together, these letters dramatize the perspectives of the two parties, as well as the tensions that characterize the relationship. As you navigate your way through the capital gap described in this chapter, it is my hope that these letters will prepare you for the possibility that your future will require outside equity investors. There is nothing more miserable for an entrepreneur than to bring in outside equity investors without some sense as to what that decision really means.

A Letter from the Investor to the Entrepreneur

May 16, 2006

Rick Wisely, PhD
CEO, Wisely Technology Partners
262 Beach Towers, Suite 4A
Virginia Beach, VA 93821

Dear Rick,

I want to start with the fact that I am honestly and sincerely excited about investing in your company. It's important for you to know that every investment that I make starts that way. I truly believe in your company's potential. I'm emotionally attached to your firm, otherwise I wouldn't back it. I believe personally in your ability to make it happen—I really don't want to manage your business—it's the last thing I want to do.

I recognize that there are a million problems a day that you fix, but I am getting a scary feeling that some of the underlying assumptions that we invested in are not playing out.

Only you know what elements we missed in our analysis. You know where the risk of failure is, and if we don't know the truth and the whole truth, our capital is not worth having. I hate to be so direct, for I don't believe you have intentionally misled us. Most entrepreneurs don't lie, but they often don't tell us everything out of fear of what we'll think. It's a sin of omission.

You should remember that I am investing other people's money; it would be easier if it were strictly my own. You're probably going to think that I go overboard about measurement, but you ought to walk a mile in my shoes. Capital is relentless. I might believe in your business, but the people I'm working for don't care about your business; all they care about is money, and they're judging me based on the math. I really do have a billion-dollar gun to my head.

I try to adopt a strategic perspective. I need to know about problems concerning the underlying assumptions about the business as early as possible, so that I have the time to help solve them, even if it takes money. Time is money for me—bigtime. I'm used to solving problems, so if one arises, tell me. That way, I can help out.

Thanks for listening.

Sincerely,

Todd P. Aldrich, IV
Managing Partner, Reginald Capital

A Letter from the Entrepreneur to the Investor

May 20, 2006

Todd,

Boy, this is a hard letter to write, honestly. I can't tell you how good it feels to finally have someone actually put real money into my company. For the first time, I feel like I have the resources I need, and that I can approach some of the decisions facing the firm without feeling that everything I own, including my firstborn, is on the line.

I guess I need to tell you that already some of the major assumptions that I made about how to grow this company are changing. I feel so compelled to stick to the story line and the plans that I truly believed existed at the time you became an investor. But things are changing. I can feel the questions coming and a sense of resentment beginning to build; I feel that if I share with you what I think is changing, you will assume I misrepresented my business from the beginning. It brings my credibility into question. I know so many details about the business, and am solving problems all the time—I am coming through a period in which I had to insulate my employees from a lot of problems just to get us all through. Remember, this business wouldn't even be here if I wasn't good at pulling rabbits out the hat without anybody's help.

I don't know which problems to insulate you from, and which to solve on my own. Going into this relationship, you're telling me that I have to trust you with what I know about the business, and I don't even know you yet. That's a scary proposition. Also, I just went through a period of time when I had to do without money. I don't know yet how to use money to solve problems, because I didn't have money to solve problems with. I'm set up to believe that if I ask you for more money, I've failed.

I have to be honest: You seem so damn busy when we get together that I don't feel like I can share the nuances. The details are important to me, but they're not important to you. You just want the big picture—you're coming at it from a higher level. How am I supposed to know which problems you want me to worry about with you?

I recognize that you have to make money for your investors. The only thing I care about is this business. I wake up worrying about satisfying the needs of the employees and customers. Also, I've got my heart and soul in this. I'm looking at this with an awareness of all the things we've done right, and all the problems we've solved, whereas it seems that you're looking at it critically, in terms of cash flow alone. Rest assured, we're building value; it's just going to take some time. You never want to hear about the stuff going right, and this makes me think that I'm not always getting the credit I deserve. How, then, do you expect me to feel free to share openly the shortcomings of the business?

Todd, I appreciated receiving your letter. Let's just let all of this stew for a bit, and maybe then sit down and reload. This has helped clear the air for me, as I hope it has for you.

Thanks,
Rick

In writing these letters, I am reminded of a lunch I had with the partner of a large private equity firm that I was cultivating as a potential customer. A former manager in one of the investment firm's portfolio companies, this partner had impressed the private equity firm's leadership so much that they had asked him to join them as an investment partner. By the time of our meeting, his role in the firm was to straighten out the firm's problem portfolio companies. As the head of a financial leadership services firm, I was meeting with him because often the first step to take when dealing with a firm's problems is to upgrade the financial leadership. Indeed, my partners are often called in to model the strategies of senior management, just as we have covered in this chapter. They are asked to determine the requirements needed to propel a business into a new profit zone.

I, too, had served as a senior executive in a portfolio company, and so the two of us hit it off. We wandered into a fascinating discussion about why, as former insiders, we thought private equity investors sometimes missed the really important major issues in due diligence.

I told him that I felt I had an unbelievable, bird's-eye view as the leader of my firm to observe the work that my partners were completing on the models of a whole lot of companies. I believed that I was seeing a sea-change shortening of the product life cycles in every business, no matter what the product or service. It was as if every company had to handle a "bet the company" transition every three to four years after the initial No Man's Land transition in order to stay aligned with the lightning-fast changes going on in a given firm's marketplace.

My lunch guest agreed, adding that what was so difficult for his firm was determining whether it was investing at the very beginning of the transition, and thus gaining the advantage of catching the company just after it had successfully realigned for growth, or whether it was investing at the end of a cycle, and thus getting stuck with helping the company during its next transition. "It's no longer just a financial engineering exercise," he remarked. "We really have to help these companies grow—management is now the key."

This last observation, it seems, goes to the essence of the difference in perspective we saw above in the fictional letters. The CEO has a pit in his stomach because he laid out a strategy that contemplated one set of circumstances, and now he or she is beginning to intuit that things are changing—and changing fast. The private equity investors, on the other hand, sense these changing circumstances based on the financial results, and are now beginning to wonder what they have invested in. It makes for some very scary times, and also for some really dysfunctional decision making.

The solution, I think, is for everyone to sit down and become radically objective about the business—to come together as partners and approach what Peter Drucker calls the "entrepreneurial art" of assessing what the "business should be" during its transitions. I think it is even more important than ever that businesses mobilize the original entrepreneur's ability to see around the corner, while at the same time, as my lunch guest so astutely observed, getting world-class management engaged in the business.

Money Pause Point Questionnaire

As we have seen, the crux of the navigational rule is the notion that reducing risk attracts capital. Let's concentrate here on the issue of risk.

1. Are there any risks in the business that can be eliminated with money?
2. Knowing all that you know about this business, would you buy it?
3. What kind of money do you really need to grow the business? Are you ready for outside equity and the transparency with investors necessary to make it work?

6

The Fifth *M*

At their inception, rapid-growth firms possess a thrilling momentum. As firms enter No Man's Land, however, this momentum evaporates, and a dangerous stagnation takes hold. To push through No Man's Land, firms must find ways to generate positive motion once again. The navigational rules examined in previous chapters are critical because in addition to the tangible benefits they bring, their implementation reinstills a sense that the firm is heading in the right direction. Yet momentum is not simply the product of the navigational rules, but also a precondition for their successful implementation. To survive No Man's Land, leaders must manage a firm's culture (i.e., its decision-making process) proactively to assure that an appearance of forward motion exists at all times, even when the firm's very survival appears uncertain.

THE POWER OF GREEN M&M's

Noodles & Company is a firm with momentum. The Boulder, Colorado–based restaurant chain has emerged as a top player in the fast casual-dining segment, with 145 locations nationwide and plans to open 28 to 35 more this year. Although the firm faces tough competition from the likes of Chipotle and Panera Bread, it has an experienced CEO who complements the vision and talents of the founder and is pursuing a clear strategic direction. A spirit of fun and creativity prevails, as evidenced by the firm's peppy and whimsical Web site (www.noodles.com) and innovations like the "Noodle News," a weekly e-mail that brings the firm's far-flung employees together by celebrating weekly successes. "There's energy here, a sense of forward motion," the firm's founder, Aaron Kennedy, remarks with a smile. "Things are really on the upswing."

They weren't always. In 2002, with the popularity of the low-carb diet, sales growth slowed to a paltry 2 percent, and the firm was having difficulty remaining relevant to consumers. Also, the experienced restaurant executive that Kennedy had brought in as the firm's CEO wasn't working out. Although Kennedy's strength had always been in branding,* the CEO was not consulting him on that aspect of the business, and the brand image was losing its edge. Constant run-ins with the CEO were making the employees miserable. "Some of the management trouble was my fault," Kennedy admits. "I had gotten really fatigued dealing with day-to-day operations, and had just wanted to be relieved of it. I wasn't monitoring the leadership situation as well as I should have been, and the whole company paid the price."

Kennedy acted forcefully to remedy the situation. Dismissing the CEO in 2003, he gathered the entire company together in one room (there were sixty corporate employees in the main office at that time) and proclaimed that Noodles & Company would chart a new course. In the months that followed, he reclaimed control over day-to-day operations, sharpened the branding, and refined the firm's

---

*Prior to starting Noodles & Company, Kennedy had handled significant product and branding responsibilities while serving as a senior executive in a major corporation. This is another case in which a new CEO did not have the foresight to integrate the entrepreneur's expertise into the business.

goals and strategy. Sensing that the firm had lost confidence in its ability to execute, he also resolved to do something fun and seemingly insignificant for the sole purpose of injecting some mojo. To celebrate St. Patrick's Day, he proclaimed that the firm would embed green M&M's in their signature, fresh made Rice Krispy Treats. "Our head of culinary services almost had a coronary," Kennedy recalls. "He said, 'We can't do this in just eight days,' but I said, 'We *are* going to do it, just to prove that we still can. This is a good idea and it's going to be fun.' And what do you know—it worked. Customers loved the dessert. To them, it looked like we were on the ball and responsive to their tastes. Internally, our success with this one small project left us with a feeling that at least we could get something new executed. That carried us. Times were tough, but we knew we weren't dead yet."

In negotiating the challenges posed by rapid growth, it is important not to neglect a firm's morale and emotional health. Tangible things such as money, experienced managers, and a workable business model are critical if a firm is to transition through No Man's Land, but they aren't enough. Entrepreneurs must also take care to sustain a sense of forward motion, or momentum, in the organization, even and especially when the firm's fortunes appear bleakest. Momentum doesn't show up on a firm's balance sheet; it isn't measurable. Yet, as we shall see, the feeling of moving forward begets actual change. For this reason, the presence or absence of this "fifth *M*" makes all the difference for a firm in the throes of transition.

UNDERSTANDING MOMENTUM

What precisely is momentum? The American Heritage dictionary defines it as "the force of motion" or "impetus in human affairs."[23] In physics, the term denotes something more precise, the mass of a body multiplied by its speed. Momentum in business is essentially comprehensible as *institutional self-esteem*. When most entrepreneurs speak of momentum, they're referring to an intangible, emotional force pushing the firm forward. They're talking about positive energy grounded in the optimistic expectation that a firm's future will be brighter than its present state.

During the start-up phase, rapid-growth firms are blessed naturally with an exhilarating sense of momentum. Many entrepreneurs leave corporations and found start-ups precisely because they hope to experience the thrilling thrust of a company taking off. Unfortunately, such momentum is difficult to sustain. As we saw in chapter 1, growth confronts firms with wrenching problems, which in turn lead to stagnation, which in turn leads to even deeper problems—and sometimes, the firm's early demise.

Just as people have difficulty embracing positive change when they lack self-esteem, so firms stagnate when stakeholders no longer feel a sense of momentum. Conversely, momentum and positive growth are closely related: Not only does growth create a wonderful sense of momentum within a firm, but that momentum in turn lays the psychological foundation for further growth to occur. To make it through No Man's Land, then, firms must generate sufficient positive energy at all times, even as they struggle to implement the navigational rules corresponding to the four Ms. At the very least, firms must sustain the *appearance* of momentum, convincing stakeholders in the deepest, darkest abyss of No Man's Land that better times are coming.

Now, hold on: I am not advocating that entrepreneurs lie to employees and fool them into believing there is momentum where none exists. I firmly believe that the most enduring source of momentum is actual forward motion, accomplished via implementation of the four Ms. Kennedy recognized this, which is why his green M&M's decision accompanied more substantive steps, such as replacement of the old CEO and formulation of a clear and comprehensive business strategy. Like all well-conceived momentum decisions, the green M&M's were in effect a stop-gap measure, a tactic undertaken to shock the culture back to life in the short term while the more tangible "four *M*" decisions were coming into effect.

But there is another, more fundamental reason why entrepreneurs cannot content themselves with pursuing the appearance of momentum. Although positive energy may be necessary for a firm's successful voyage through No Man's Land, it is by no means sufficient. As previous chapters have argued, a firm must have a business model that scales, competent management, sufficient finances, and alignment with customers, or it will never make it to a profitable adulthood.

Yet if self-esteem is no substitute for implementing the navigational rules associated with the four *M*s, successful implementation of the four *M*s also requires that a certain amount of momentum already exist. Momentum galvanizes an organization, reconciles it to wrenching change, even allows such change to go forward when mistakes are made and readjustment becomes necessary mid-course. Momentum transforms the firm into a speeding locomotive, confronting stakeholders with a stark choice: Get onboard, or get out of the way. Decisions relating to the four *M*s are frequently difficult and counterintuitive, but they are far easier for stakeholders to accept when the sense of forward movement is palpable.

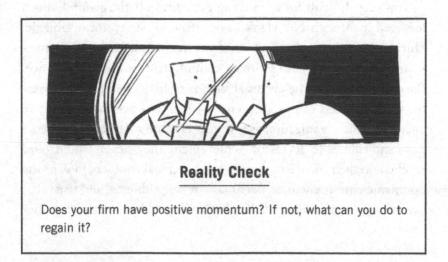

Reality Check

Does your firm have positive momentum? If not, what can you do to regain it?

Cultivating Momentum: A Leader's Handbook

Years ago, one of my partners asked me to summarize the key leadership traits and abilities of a great CEO. I shuddered at the task, thinking that this was like trying to boil down the history of the world into a few concise paragraphs. I still can't imagine how one might reduce great leadership across companies and industries to a single bullet-point list. At the same time, I have learned that one characteristic surely belongs on that list: the ability of all great leaders to generate and sustain organizational momentum.

Now, how does a leader sustain the feeling of positive energy? There is no single rule or set of rules. The manner in which momentum is cultivated will be influenced by the specific qualities of an individual's leadership style. Green M&M's might work in one organizational context; it won't necessarily work in another. Still, it is possible to describe some general levers that leaders of emerging growth firms in No Man's Land can pull to create momentum in their organizations.

Lever #1: Optimism

It is very difficult for a leader to get a firm off the ground, much less lead it through No Man's Land, if he or she is not optimistic. During the start-up phase, most of the momentum in a firm derives from the entrepreneur's own commitment and self-sacrifice. Buoyed by belief in the eventual success of his or her vision, the entrepreneur infects others with enthusiasm, thus generating positive energy for the organization as a whole. Day after day, entrepreneurs push individuals to levels of achievement they never would have reached on their own. Employees and other stakeholders look to the optimistic entrepreneur to personally solve problems, and trust that the entrepreneur will never let the firm's problems get him or her down.

No Man's Land pushes an entrepreneur's emotional resilience to its limits. It's difficult to stay optimistic when your customers are complaining, your managers are over their heads, and you have no idea how you are going to make payroll. As Heidi Gerding, CEO of the government IT contractor HeiTech Services, remarks, "No Man's Land is depressing. I wake up scared every morning, thinking to myself, Oh, my God, today I have to go to work and figure out what we are going to do to replace a contract that is going to end next year. I lie awake worrying about when the right management will arrive to help me grow. I'm so afraid of failure, of waking up one morning and finding my contacts aren't here and I don't have a business anymore."

And yet, as Gerding knows, you simply cannot let such concerns get the better of you. Do whatever it takes, but don't lose the determination, hopefulness, and can-do attitude that your employees have come to depend on. When times get tough, Gerding finds it helpful to turn to her husband for moral support and mentoring. Also, she and her business partner make sure to take personal days from time to time to keep sane. "There are times when I just can't bear to come in," she remarks. "My partner, too. So what we do is give ourselves permission to go off by ourselves to get some breathing room. We regain our balance and then things don't seem so threatening anymore."

Over the long term, entrepreneurs should also sustain optimism by attempting to delegate some of the burden of the organization's emotional health. As we saw in chapter 2, rapid-growth firms that pass through No Man's Land establish impersonal systems for delivering on the entrepreneur's value proposition. Something similar must also be developed in relation to the firm's emotional health. After No Man's Land, the firm's broader leadership layer has to shoulder the burden of generating optimism throughout the organization. At General Electric, for instance, a perception reigns within the culture that there is enough talent to solve any problem that may arise in the firm's diverse portfolio of businesses. As an entrepreneur, you need to get to where GE is.

The sooner you can institutionalize the resilience and creativity you use to face down adversity, the easier it will be to keep even the lowest employees feeling positive. I am not, of course, suggesting that entrepreneurs should institutionalize false optimism based on a blind faith in the company's prospects. Rather, what entrepreneurs are uniquely suited to provide is optimism based on their own business visions. Unlike other employees in the firm, entrepreneurs have the capacity to "see around the corner"; they can discern opportunity even when none appears to exist. Furthermore, as creative people, entrepreneurs tend instinctively to emphasize possibilities rather than obstacles. It is this visionary optimism, founded on intuition, that requires systematization as the firm grows.

Lever #2: Clarify the Decision-Making Process

How are decisions made in your firm? Who makes the tough calls, and according to which values? What are the firm's overarching goals and ambitions?

As we discussed in chapter 3, a clear and successful pattern of decision making defines a firm's culture. Yet such a pattern is also essential to maintaining momentum within that culture. After all, it's very difficult to feel a sense of forward motion if decisions seem capricious and irrational, or if employees have only an ambiguous sense of what a firm is trying to accomplish.

In setting up shop, most entrepreneurs intuitively establish a set of company objectives, and in turn personally become the very center of the decision-making process. As layers of management are added and the model is scaled up, the risk is that the firm's original values, sense of mission, and visionary voices will be lost. The entrepreneur's and the new outside manager's challenge within No Man's Land is thus to think more consciously about the firm's culture, and to take steps to clarify, simplify, and build confidence in the company's decision-making process.

A View from the Trenches

Doug Groves, CEO, Carapace LLC

"As a family business, we have had trouble at various times with maintaining clarity. When family distributors fail, often it is because there are a bunch of owners with different energy levels, different risk thresholds, and, most important, different ideas of what the strategy should be. When I took over the business, I wanted us to go after a new product line in a big way, and a longtime manager within the firm didn't like it. We had to resolve that before moving forward, and we did resolve it. This clarification was a huge change. All of a sudden, people in our firm knew where the buck stopped and what the strategy was. It became fun to work there again."

Can large firms retain a strong and clear sense of purpose? Sure. As evidence, compare how decisions are made at two large corporations, General Electric and AIG. At General Electric, it's the results that count, and decisions in each business must satisfy a famous criterion: Will they help the business become first or second in its industry? At AIG, by contrast, decision making long centered on strict personal accountability to AIG's founder, Hank Greenberg. As one executive once told me, "Whatever I do I can't lose Mr. Greenberg's money."

"You mean on a portfolio basis?" I asked.

"No," he said. "I mean I can't lose Mr. Greenberg's money on *any* deal."[24]

General Electric and AIG: two large companies, two very different cultures, yet two equally clear decision-making patterns.

Due to their relatively small size, fast-growth companies are in an excellent position to protect employees' confidence in the decision-making process. The next time you step into a meeting, think about your firm's culture (i.e., its decision-making process). Do folks really have confidence in the way decisions are being made? You will never be able to generate momentum if that confidence breaks down.

Lever #3: Give the Organization a Kick in the Pants

The previous two approaches tend to generate momentum slowly and on an ongoing basis. Sometimes a firm's culture has stagnated for so long that it requires something dramatic—an action or event that signifies a clear rupture with the past. If your firm is flatlining, don't wait for a doctor to show up and proclaim it dead; instead, fire up the defibrillator and march onward using the following three methods:

SHAKE UP THE INNER CIRCLE OF DECISION MAKERS

An easy way to give your firm an immediate momentum rush is to shake up the inner circle. Every entrepreneur surrounds him- or herself with a small group of key advisers and decision makers. To employees and customers, the makeup of this circle defines the culture more powerfully than any videotape, newsletter, memo, or meeting ever can. If you don't believe me, consider this: Even the lowest employee in your firm can probably name without hesitation the members of your trusted coterie. Shaking up the inner circle is thus a powerful gesture. Beyond allowing for a freshness of vision, influx of new DNA into the inner circle signals to the entire company that important changes have been made, new perspectives are being heard, and it's time for employees to roll up their sleeves and have faith again.

Even when crisis is not beckoning, entrepreneurs should treat their inner circle as a momentum lever. American presidents do exactly that, populating their executive teams so as to send clear messages about policy choices and priorities and in this way create a sense of momentum behind the president's agenda. As an entrepreneur, you can expand your circle of confidants, contract it, diversify it, homogenize it. Whatever you do, the important thing is that you *manage* it. In my company, I decided for strategic reasons to maintain an inner circle that was larger and more inclusive than is commonly the case. I continued, of course, to select members of my inner circle purposefully, so that the symbolic power of the selection remained intact. At the same time, I made sure that I maintained some continuity in my inner circle alongside the flux. It's incredibly important not to send the message that your inner circle is dominated by the new voices in the leadership. The leadership of an emerging growth business should always retain some of the original voices; in this way, it can maintain employees' confidence that the right people are being listened to about the right issues.

Do something radical

In basketball, coaches typically call trick plays or switch players in and out just to jar the team a bit and fire up players' expectations of success. Likewise, in No Man's Land the sense of stagnation is sometimes so debilitating that you have to make a move for the sole purpose of creating momentum. So embrace green M&M's. Or red ones. Or Reese's Pieces. Do something fun—whatever it takes to inject life into the firm. Don't worry about the decision's financial ramifications, or whether the decision is logical, or whether the decision is in strict keeping with the financial or business model. The point is simply to prove that your firm has mojo and can still solve a problem. As one entrepreneur has told me, "You always have to move the ball forward."

To consider just how far some entrepreneurs are willing to go to move the ball forward, consider the following story from Cameron Garrison. As we saw in chapter 4, Garrison's firm, Garrison Enterprises, initially made money by selling newsletter subscriptions about health-code violations. Anticipating changes to his market, Garrison abruptly switched models, getting into the business of selling records-management software to health departments. In making the switch, Garrison managed to steer his firm through a six-month transitional period of zero revenue. After the transition was complete, however, Garrison's firm went through a period of slackening momentum. To remedy the situation, he made a spontaneous, and rather expensive, purchase for a key employee who really needed a lift. I'll let him tell the story:

> Our business stalled when we had seven people. I'd been pushing them way too hard. We started making stupid mistakes that the customers were picking up on. So what I started doing was "bribing" the employees to freshen them up. I started sharing more of the wealth, giving them cash in some instances, and also doing things like sending one of the key guys to Disneyland with his family for a few days.
>
> On one occasion, I was driving back from Atlanta with our chief technology officer. He had slept like all of six hours in the past six weeks. We passed a BMW dealership. I knew that his dream was to have a roadster. I pulled off at the dealership. He thought we were just looking. We took a Z4 for a test drive. Then I bought it for him, just like that.
>
> It was the craziest thing I've ever done in my life, but it paid off. My CTO told me later that this one thing got him through. Every morning after a long night, he would get into the car and just driving it would remind him of why he was doing what he was doing and that it was making a difference in his life. For four hundred dollars a month, I got a half million dollars in extra work. You can't pocket all the money yourself. You have to find a way to help those around you feel that they've grown personally as well.

Bo Burlingham points out that "reminding people in unexpected ways how much the company cares about them" is an important means of creating "a culture of intimacy." A culture of intimacy is indeed a wonderful thing, but, as Garrison found, such unexpected reminders can also have a more direct, instrumental value; they can serve to stimulate momentum just at the moment when a growing firm needs it most.[25]

MESS UP THE BUSINESS (AND THEN CLEAN IT UP)

Sometimes momentum decisions can change the very face of a firm. Bindographics is a large, family-owned firm headquartered in Baltimore that provides printers with a range of binding and finishing services, such as hole punching, tabs, and folding. The firm was hit hard in 2001 by the aftereffects of 9/11 and the dot-com bust. Although revenues soon recovered, it became clear to Marty Anson, Bindographics's CEO, that the firm needed a major change of direction to sustain momentum and keep the business viable for Anson's sons to take over.

Since binding is a mature industry, Anson tinkered with the idea of making a move outside his industry. He kept his eyes out for an acquisition, and in 2005 purchased Kolad, a printing business in Buffalo, New York, that specialized in information packaging. One year later, Kolad's acquisition has pushed Bindographics's total revenues to the $30 million mark and offered wonderful new opportunities for creativity in the business. With Kolad's revenues poised to grow to $50 million in the years to come, Bindographics has much more momentum than it did before, to the point where Anson's sons are excited about taking over the firm.

As we saw in chapter 3, and as Bindographics's experience suggests, "messing up" a business entails making promises to customers that you haven't made before, whether by taking on new customers or by serving new needs of existing customers. Making new promises generates momentum because it forces the firm to change its internal processes so as to meet those promises. Employees and others within the firm are confronted with the need to be creative and adopt new solutions, and as they prove that they can do these things, positive energy takes hold.

Many entrepreneurs feel guilty about messing up the business, since they know they are creating new hassles for their employees. Yet, as we saw earlier, if a firm doesn't make new promises from time to time, it is stuck with stagnant customers and runs the risk of dying a slow, cancerous death. If the firm makes too many promises, excessive burdens are placed on the firm's staff members, and the firm is never able to "clean up" by developing the processes required to meet customer needs. Rather than a slow, cancerous death, the firm crashes and burns.

What firms really need is not "messing up" or "cleaning up" but a productive *balance* between the two.

One caveat, though. Although entrepreneurs should not shrink from making new customer promises, they should take care to do so *purposefully*. Remember, some promises lead to whole rooms full of new customers, whereas others lead to an empty room with only a couple of new customers in it. Beyond renewed momentum, entrepreneurs need to make sure that the promises they make in "messing up" the company open up long-term opportunities for the firm. In Bindographics's case, the acquisition of Kolad made sense for a number of reasons. Kolad was sound, it was purchased at auction for a good price, and it was in an industry related to Bindographics's existing business. Most important, Anson felt confident, based on his own extensive knowledge of the business, that demand for Kolad's products would grow in the years to come. As a result, he got exactly what he bargained for: a roomful of new customers, as well as an influx of positive energy.

The Case of Lincoln Logistics

Anson could sustain momentum because he enjoyed latitude in determining how to "mess up" the business. He had a license to think creatively, and the authority, when the time was right, to move his organization in a new direction. Not all entrepreneurs are so lucky.

Rich Lincoln is CEO of Lincoln Logistics,[26] a family-owned firm founded in 1920 and based in Charleston, South Carolina. The firm provides freight forwarding, customs clearance, and the purchase of shipping and air cargo space for both importers and exporters. It has grown steadily in recent years, from about $5 million in revenues during the early 1990s to about $10 million in 2006. However, like

First Standard Freight, Inc., the New York, New York–based freight forwarder we encountered in chapter 1, Lincoln has struggled with tight margins and competition from large multinational corporations. Globalization has increased demand across the board, but the industry has become stratified between corporate giants at the top and thousands of small mom-and-pop operations with less than $1 million in revenues at the bottom. "For mid-sized firms like ours, it's tough, a nickel-and-dime business," Rich Lincoln says. "The fees we charge haven't risen much in recent years."

To improve margins, Lincoln has moved into the slightly more lucrative business of buying shipping space and reselling it at a profit to customers. Yet this has increased significantly the level of risk. Rich Lincoln now has to maintain a network of agents around the world and invest capital up front to buy the space at wholesale. "Our model is changing," he says. "Our business used to be essentially a transaction business; we acted as agents for merchants and manufacturers seeking to ship goods, and charged fixed fees. Now we have to put up a significant amount of capital. One mistake, one problem with a customer account, and we're hurting. To make matters worse, the corporate guys started extending credit to customers to buy shipping space, so now we have to. To bring in ten million dollars in revenues, we need to bill out a hundred million dollars. It's killing our margins."

Thanks to significant IT investments, Lincoln can still keep pace with the services offered by corporate players. The firm can even offer a compelling value proposition in the form of better reliability and customer service. Yet as Rich Lincoln has had to acknowledge, it may not be possible to make money as a mid-sized firm for much longer. "In the mid-1990s, I spoke with a guy who worked for a national company that was acquiring regional firms like mine. I remember him saying, 'You either have to get in the game like us, or you're going to shrink and become a mom-and-pop again.' And that's the choice we face. We have to move somewhere to survive. We can't stand still."

Lincoln thinks the answer is to get bigger through acquisitions and organic sales. The problem he faces, though, is getting the firm's shareholders—his own family members—to agree to invest. "Some of our owners are elderly aunts and cousins of mine who depend on their annual share of company profits to live off of. I only own five percent of the company. I can't tell you how hard it is to convince them that times aren't what they used to be, that we need to take bold steps to move ahead or there may not *be* a business in a few years."

For years now, the firm has put off committing to a new direction, and as a result it is stagnating. To make the best of the situation, Rich Lincoln has tried to build momentum by taking a number of smaller steps. After forming an executive task force on innovation, he decided to focus on matching the offerings of corporate competitors and positioning Lincoln Logistics as a full-service regional firm. The firm is exploring some potentially lucrative customer niches, has invested heavily in bulking up its sales force, and has significantly increased its ability to rapidly deploy IT to solve customer problems. Yet Rich Lincoln is frustrated. "Doing all these little things is great, but at the end of the day, we need to expand our footprint. I'm handicapped by my owners. I need capital to get big, but I can't withstand the family pressure. I feel a sense of vertigo, and to tell you the truth, there are times when it is a bit difficult to stay positive about the business's future."

. . .

In this chapter, we've introduced the concept of momentum and provided some general guidelines as to how entrepreneurs in No Man's Land can rekindle or sustain it. In cases where there is very little an entrepreneur can do to generate momentum, the long-term prognosis for the firm is not bright. Getting through No Man's Land is a bet-the-company commitment. You can't both move to scale and not move to scale. A growing firm can survive for some time in a stagnant state, but not indefinitely. Something has to be done, and no number of half-measures, however well intentioned, will suffice.

For Rich Lincoln, the only option now is to sit down with other stakeholders and have an honest discussion about what the firm is about, and what it could look like going forward. Is it worthwhile to take Lincoln Logistics through No Man's Land? Should the company be sold or scaled back?

When it is no longer possible to generate momentum, the firm is at a crossroads, and entrepreneurs need to start reevaluating the path toward growth. Rich Lincoln knows this, and he is heartbroken—you can see it on his face. Yet the reality might not be as bad as he thinks. Growth is exciting, but foregoing it—whether by staying small or by selling out to someone else—is not necessarily a personal tragedy. As we shall see in the next chapter, the decision to grow is ultimately a complex one that takes into account the entrepreneur's personal goals as well as the firm's financial prospects. Whether you're running a venerable family firm or a young firm you've built from scratch, sometimes the most responsible, most fulfilling, and most lucrative thing you can do in the face of No Man's Land is simply to back off.

7

Beyond Growth

Should a firm get big? There is no "correct" answer. The decision to embark on the No Man's Land journey—or to complete the journey once it has already begun—reflects not merely an assessment of the firm's financial prospects or its ability to apply the four Ms, but also a determination of the entrepreneur's own personal ambitions. Leading a firm after it has passed through No Man's Land requires standing back and taking on an investor's perspective. To achieve true success, entrepreneurs must look into their hearts and assess whether running the business in a way satisfactory to investors is consistent with their deepest values and dreams.

PRATER'S DILEMMA

By this point in the book, perhaps you've thought through the four Ms and are reasonably sure that you can guide your business through No Man's Land. You think you can execute the market, management, model, and money navigational rules, while maintaining enough momentum to see you through the tough times. The question remains:

Should you grow? Are the benefits of working through No Man's Land always worth the tremendous costs? And what does the future look like after No Man's Land?

As we saw in chapter 1, there are essentially three possible endgames, aside from going out of business, awaiting a firm that survives No Man's Land. The entrepreneur can continue to drive the firm to maturity, managing the institutional processes set up to deliver the value proposition. In this case, the entrepreneur either (1) builds a self-sustaining enterprise, or (2) sells and helps fuel an established, larger company, serving as that firm's de facto R&D. Alternately, the entrepreneur can decide to pare back the firm. Offering customers value derived from his or her own personal efforts and talents, the entrepreneur establishes the firm as a "small giant"—a company focused on the quality of its offerings rather than on its size.

Deciding whether to grow, then, amounts to assessing the business's potential and determining which of these three options best suits the entrepreneur's own interests and capabilities. To illustrate the complexity of the choice, and to introduce a plan for addressing it, I'd like to develop in more detail the story of one entrepreneur I know, Burt Prater. As we saw in the introduction, Prater left a thriving medical practice to found the medical surveillance firm EMR. By providing a standardized protocol for medical exams, subcontracting the exams out to local medical clinics, and then compiling exam results into customized medical reports, EMR helped its clients, the health and safety compliance officers at environmental remediation firms, satisfy government regulations mandating regular medical monitoring of their firms' employees. Rapid growth ensued. By 1995, five years after its founding, EMR had sixty employees and $4 million to $5 million in revenues. With a network of almost one thousand local medical clinics in place, it was overseeing two hundred thousand exams a year and claimed a market share of more than 50 percent.

Yet EMR was at a crossroads. Its core business was commodifying;

margins were shrinking, and the firm was poised to lose its largest customer—representing 20 percent of revenues—to a lower-priced competitor. "We provided great service and expertise," Prater remembers. "As the industry pioneer, we'd created the right protocols and had developed an exam kit that even an idiot could use. Our quality was top-notch. The local doctors we worked with were top-notch. But this model was easy to duplicate. Our competitors were intercepting our kits and the forms we were using, then undercutting our prices."

As Prater now realizes, EMR was in No Man's Land, struggling with challenges posed by the market M. "We'd grown out of alignment with customer needs," Prater says.

> At first our customers were the health and safety executives at the environmental firms. These guys didn't care about cost; they wanted quality exams and customized services and protocols that were unique to their particular company yet consistently applied in all the local areas where the company operated. Yet by the mid-1990s, Superfund money was drying up, and this put the squeeze on our customer firms. All of a sudden, the CFOs at these firms were our clients, and they didn't care about customization. They just wanted compliance with government regulations at the lowest cost.

When EMR started, the firm was billing out medical exams at nine hundred dollars apiece. Now, with commodification, the price per exam was coming down to the three hundred-dollar range.

Prater wasn't sure what to do, but he sensed that extricating his firm from No Man's Land required realigning it to get ahead of the commodification trend. "Commodification wasn't necessarily a threat," he says.

> If that's the way the industry was moving, the path toward growth was to lead the charge. We would have to listen to our customers and bring costs down to the bare bottom, even if this meant compromising on the customized services that we were

so good at designing for each company. We would negotiate tough new exam rates with our local docs and cut out all the frills in the services we provide. In the end, we could increase our volume, bring down our prices, and protect our margins.

Prater was reasonably sure he could succeed at implementing the four *M*s and growing his core business. His gut told him that once realigned his firm would become highly attractive as a target for acquisition. Yet Prater had other opportunities. For the last two years, EMR had been pursuing a whole new kind of customer, a Fortune 50 firm that was exploring whether to outsource all of its health and safety operations. If this deal closed, EMR would double its revenues overnight and establish a foothold in an exciting new industry. With five years of revenue guaranteed under this new contract, EMR could milk its medical surveillance business under its existing model for as long as possible, while aggressively going after more outsourcing business from other Fortune 50 firms.

Prater had spent $1 million gearing up for the Fortune 50 client and was excited about the contract. Yet he nursed lingering doubts. On the one hand, Prater would have to take on millions of dollars in new capital in order to hire staff and make infrastructure changes necessary to serve the Fortune 50 client. To obtain the capital, he would need to part with considerable equity in EMR. Also, during eighteen months of negotiation and preparatory work on the part of EMR, the Fortune 50 firm had rewritten the contract several times, placing more and more performance burdens on Prater's firm. As Prater was coming to realize, the client wanted to outsource, yet was determined to maintain complete control. Depending on how several variables played out, there was a real chance that the contract would lock EMR into a painful and contentious client relationship down the road.

Two weeks before the closing date, two things happened that threw the deal into tumult and Prater into a painful crisis. Final scrutiny of the venture capital contracts revealed that Prater would lose majority ownership of the firm if the deal went through. Meanwhile, his largest customer, representing 20 percent of revenues, called and announced that it was putting EMR's business up for competitive bid. The customer had a company that was willing to handle its surveillance needs for less than two hundred dollars an exam—less than EMR's own cost. Would EMR meet the price?

Prater was floored. Before, his firm had seemed in a pretty good position to weather the challenges before it, but now he was confronted with a stark choice. If he met this new price, all of his other customers would expect similar price cuts. To stay profitable, he'd have to push ahead with market realignment immediately and at full force. Yet he couldn't succeed at this and accept the outsourcing contract at the same time. The outsourcing contract involved a wholesale reorientation and remaking of the firm; it would require his full attention. It was either one or the other. "How does one make a decision like that?" he asks. "I told my wife: This is the toughest call I've ever had to make."

LOOKING INWARD

As Prater discovered, the decision to grow can be especially wrenching when it is impossible to discern with any clarity whether growth is "best" for the business. Often, in fact, either path—growing or retreating—can carry attendant risks and benefits that seem about equal. In these cases, the decision to grow becomes an intensely personal one. Why did you start the business in the first place? What do you hope to get out of it? These are the kinds of questions entrepreneurs need to pose if they are to determine a course of action that they will be able to live with over the long term.

When queried on the desirability of growth, the entrepreneurs interviewed for this book took strongly diverging views. Some expressed a determination to grow, no matter what the cost. "It's very simple," one entrepreneur remarked. "The first billion takes it. We're going to grow this thing because we believe it has that kind of potential." Heidi Gerding, president and CEO of HeiTech Services, notes that she often puts on an investor's hat, because she wants to know how much the business is worth. This in turn relates to her ambition: "The decisions we're making now are really going to decide whether we survive or fail. For us, there is no option of staying small. My idea of success is to run a company with name recognition. I had always wanted my name on the side of a building, on a billboard. I would never consider myself a success if I were small."

Other entrepreneurs expressed a need to innovate or lead, which in turn strongly influenced their decision to grow or contract. By the early 2000s, David Stone's firm, Kensington Glass Arts, had grown to $4 million in revenues by providing high-quality etched and frosted glass to commercial and high-end residential clients. He took a big gamble to get into a slightly different business—glass fabrication—not because he aspired to make more money or become famous, but because he was bored and wanted to do something different. Likewise, Tom Lynch was determined to expand his firm, Infinity Software Development, into different cities because he couldn't imagine doing otherwise—he loved the firm and loved to lead.

John Tripodi was so committed to his initial vision that in selecting his firm's endgame, he focused most determinedly on the alternative that would best enable his vision to shine. Describing his decision to sell his business, Heritage Information Systems, he explains that anticipated changes in his customer base meant that his vision would stand a better chance of surviving as part of a larger company. "I had no problem with selling," he said. "I'd always felt that I could walk away. I've won the game. The object of the game was to build wealth and be honest to my vision. So now that I've gotten both, I have no problem getting out. My vision will continue and I got paid what I thought it was worth. Without that, I'd still be running it."

Some entrepreneurs, such as Glen Davidson of PATLive, have little interest in running their company's day-to-day operations, yet are able to transition to a strategic role and remain fulfilled by contributing to their company's creative product-development cycle. The point, again, is that there is no "correct" answer as to whether a firm should grow.

For entrepreneurs who find the idea of running a large firm distasteful, the correct solution might be to grow the business to a certain size, then sell. Another alternative is to shrink the business and run it by themselves or with the help of a few trusted employees. After spending the bulk of this book providing a framework for growth, I'd like to remove the stigma that exists around staying small once and for all. It's neither illegal, unethical, nor nonsensical to forego scale and keep the business organized around your own personal efforts. Some world-class chefs, for instance, are perfectly happy becoming fully engaged emotionally and financially with one restaurant rather than leveraging that restaurant into a national brand. They enjoy a chance to engage in a simple way with their customers and employees. They retain their autonomy, and can adjust their businesses in ways that are most interesting and fulfilling to them.

Staying small is a risky proposition in that you don't have an organization to fall back on beyond your personal efforts. Also, since a small business is based on your personal efforts, its value is limited, since it almost certainly will not survive you. Finally, not all businesses are susceptible to staying small. In Burt Prater's case, there probably was little future for EMR if it could not scale up and compete on price. Yet for entrepreneurs who can stay small, who wish to lead, and who regard the risks and pressures of running a larger company as something less than a "promised land," staying small might represent the perfect solution—if only these entrepreneurs would give it a chance.

In making the final call on whether to grow, some entrepreneurs mistakenly rely on a superficial analysis or on a vaguely understood "gut instinct." In Prater's case, it was tempting to deemphasize his core business and go with the Fortune 50 contract. "Here I am, this little country boy from Alabama who has put together a concept that happened to work, and all of a sudden I have a Fortune 50 company that's giving me a thirty-million-dollar contract. That's pretty damn neat. If you're going on ego, it's a no-brainer."

Yet, to his credit, Prater did not go with "ego." What he did, essentially, was look inward in accordance with a fairly rigorous two-step analysis. The first step was to determine what his *personal future as a leader* would look like if he decided to grow his core business. The second was to determine what the *personal economic implications* of growing or not growing might be.

Let's begin with the first step: What does the entrepreneur's leadership role look like after No Man's Land? We've already laid out what a *firm* looks like after No Man's Land. It has happy customers, a huge potential for growth, a confident and capable management team, a clear and viable business model, access to free-flowing capital, and, not least, a culture that is alive with a feeling of positive movement. Yet the entrepreneur's emotional future in this endgame is not the same as the firm's. It is quite possible for a firm to blossom after No Man's Land, while its founders find themselves stressed-out and miserable. Even with the firm on relatively stable footing, there are always business challenges for entrepreneurs to face, and there is always competition. More fundamentally, after No Man's Land entrepreneurs find themselves grappling with a host of challenges, including the next realignment transition that needs to be made for the company to remain on its growth path.

Most entrepreneurs start companies because they want to work for themselves. As their companies grow, entrepreneurs come to realize that they are responsible for a whole new constituency: their employees. When entrepreneurs make it through No Man's Land, however, they might also become responsible for pleasing a third constituency, their equity partners. To meet this responsibility, they must force themselves to look at the business from a radically different perspective, that of the *investor*. They must allocate resources ruthlessly so as to maximize return on investment. No longer is the business a personal project of the entrepreneur's creation; it's an asset subject to the impersonal laws of economics.

In deciding whether or not to grow, entrepreneurs need to determine what precisely the adoption of an investor's perspective will mean for how they run their businesses. Will the imperative to maximize returns require that the entrepreneur lay off trusted employees, or otherwise treat them in a manner inconsistent with his or her values? Will it require that the firm develop product lines in which the entrepreneur is personally uninterested? Will it require that the entrepreneur spend most of his or her time working on the business rather than on new ideas, or vice versa? And then the ultimate question: Can the entrepreneur live with and thrive under these and other eventualities?

In addition to imagining what the experience of running the business from the point of view of investor returns would entail, entrepreneurs need to take on the point of view of an investor *right now* and calculate whether they and their current shareholders would benefit more from growth or from choosing another endgame option. Sometimes this calculation itself is enough to help the entrepreneur decide whether or not to grow.

In Prater's case, the economic calculus loomed especially large. Prater knew that running the business from the investor's perspective would require that he once again take on the role of entrepreneur, building a business in a new industry. Although Prater had enjoyed running his business, he didn't feel the kind of intense inner drive to lead and innovate that many entrepreneurs feel. He could imagine himself starting out fresh but thought that, all things being equal, he might be just as happy sticking with the business he already had, growing it, then cashing out within twenty-four months. But would all things be equal in financial terms? Or did Prater stand to make out far better going for it, taking the capital available to him and expanding the outsourcing business?

On a superficial level, going with the Fortune 50 firm seemed to be the right move, despite its risks. Certainly the venture capitalists were strongly behind it. As they saw it, EMR had the potential to grow to $200 million or more if it diversified its business. Upon closer inspection, however, there was serious question as to how much Prater would personally benefit, given his reduced stake in the firm.

To illustrate the importance and complexity of calculating the entrepreneur's financial endgame scenarios, let's go through Prater's own analysis step-by-step:

Step 1: Burt was faced with two basic scenarios—reorganize his core business and drive it to a low-cost offering that made money, or take on the new big outsourcing contract. The problem with the second scenario was that it required more money. Figure 1 shows the impact the new contract would have on Burt's business's revenues.

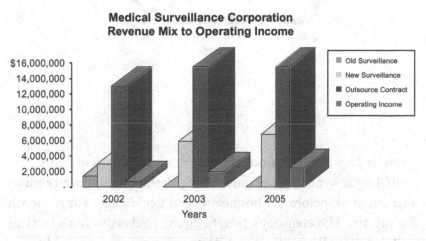

Figure 1

Notice that revenues from the new outsourcing business—the third bars—hover around the $15 million range, and revenue from the new revamped medical surveillance business increases into the $7 million to $8 million range by 2005. As you can see from the fourth bars, representing operating income, the business overall ramps up nicely and makes some money. So far, so good, right?

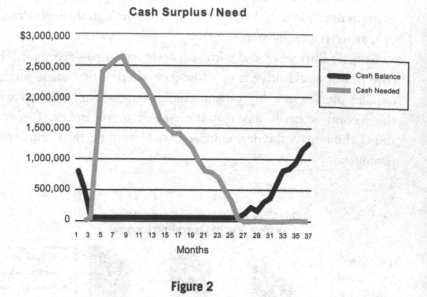

Figure 2

Step 2: Not so fast. Look at the cash requirements in figure 2.

If Prater went with the outsourcing deal, he would need cash to make it work before the business began generating cash at month twenty-six. The company's private equity backers were more than willing to give Prater the money, but as we saw earlier, the additional investment would cost Prater control of the company.

Step 3: Now look at how the previous two schedules would look if Burt walked from the outsourcing deal and concentrated only on getting his old product revamped into a new, cheaper, more stream-lined product:

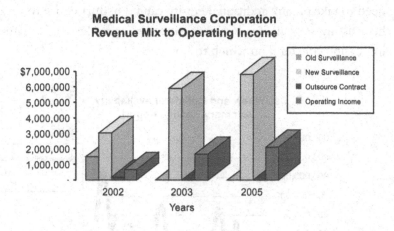

Figure 3. A smaller business but very profitable

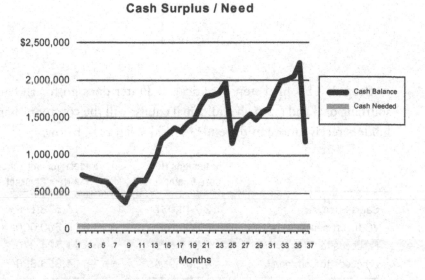

Figure 4. Not to mention a healthy cash surplus

In addition, as you can see from figure 5 below, there would be no need to take on any additional equity capital if Burt chose to revamp his existing surveillance business, since he would have adequate and increasing collateral on which to borrow:

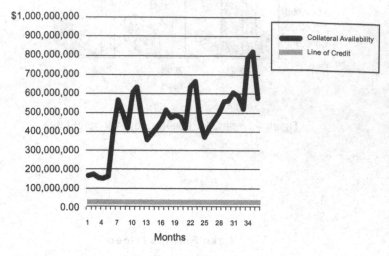

Cash Flow and Collateral Availability: Summary Results Report

Figure 5

Step 4: This final step is critical. If Prater does go for the outsourcing deal and takes on additional equity, will the common shareholders receive more in the end? Consider figure 6, below:

	Redesigns His Core Business	Redesigns and Takes the New Contract
Sales Price	12,742,037	16,578,196
VC Investment	3,500,000	6,500,000
Proceeds to VC	8,379,823	11,724,370
Proceeds to Common	4,362,214	4,853,826

Figure 6

The numbers in this figure are based on a sales price of six times EBITDA. Taking a look at the left-hand column, notice how much the common shareholders would have received if Burt walked away from the deal and redesigned his business to be smaller and more profitable. Compare that to how much the common shareholders would have gotten if he took the venture capital money and sold a much larger, more diversified business for a slightly higher multiple (seven times EBITDA).[27]

As Burt realized, he wouldn't drive much more wealth for his team and the common shareholders if he went with the outsourcing deal over the same period of time. Of course, he couldn't predict the future. It is possible that other large contracts might have followed if he went the outsourcing route, and that the payoff to all participants would have been bigger than in figure 6. The key thing to realize, though, is that Burt gained substantial insight by considering the economic ramifications of the various endgame options available to him. He learned that despite appearances, creation of a larger company via the outsourcing route did not necessarily leave him and other common shareholders very far ahead.

MAKING THE CALL

So what did Prater decide? He anguished over it, ran through the pros and cons of each path again and again, and in the end decided to disregard what his private equity backers were saying and instead turn to focus on his core business. "I just wasn't comfortable with the risks of the outsourcing deal. I liked running my own business, but the last thing I wanted to do was work for someone else—in this case, my private equity backers, or even the Fortune 50 company, which was placing ever more restrictions on my freedom of motion." In making the decision, Prater drew upon his deepest beliefs and values. "My father used to tell me that one thing you should never, ever do is work for someone else. Try to be your own boss in business, your own master. That's a big reason why I went to medical school in the first place. For me, it was easier to sell the business than work for someone else."

The immediate aftermath of the decision was tough. "I'll never forget what it was like to call the executives at the Fortune 50 firm and tell them that I was backing out. You have to understand—they had already announced internally that the deal was happening. This was a big thing for them. The doctors on their staff that we were supposed to be taking on were hugely disappointed—they wanted to work for us!"

After calling off the deal, Prater and his executive team got down to work. They restructured the core medical surveillance business, streamlined it, grew the revenues to $10 million, and led the industry in price competitiveness. Twenty months later, the business was sold, and everyone, including the company's private equity firm, made money. "I made out quite well," Prater reports. "Of course, we'll never know how much money I could have made. But today I'm certain that I made the right call. With something like this, your personal philosophy of life has to drive it. I was alone when I got into this thing, and I was alone when I got out. There are tons of reasons to make decisions, but not all of them are financial in nature."

I couldn't have said it better myself.

8

A National Treasure

Our economy's strength does not owe primarily to large corporations or to small businesses, but to the presence in most industries of innovative firms that experience explosive growth. Unfortunately, policy makers seldom treat growth firms as the national treasures they quite literally are. To sustain and improve this country's economic performance, we must change government policies that unduly prejudice emerging growth firms. Granted a level playing field, emerging growth firms will thrive, improving our competitiveness in world markets and ensuring America's continued prosperity.

WHAT'S GOING ON HERE?

Mac Sullivan is used to tough competition in the food service business, but he never thought he'd have to contend with his state and local governments as well.

Founded in 1885, Sullivan's family firm, Pate Dawson, has withstood competition from industry goliaths such as Sysco ($32 billion in 2006 revenue) to grow from about $25 million in revenue in the

1990s to almost a quarter billion dollars today. Since Sullivan took over in the early 1990s, Pate Dawson has moved away from serving independent school districts and taken on larger restaurant chains as customers. As we saw in chapter 2, Pate Dawson has leveraged this chain business to develop an entirely new, relationship-based model for servicing independent restaurants. Whereas most distributors try to profit from small restaurants' lack of buying sophistication, Pate Dawson takes these businesses on as equal partners, building trust by sharing its own business model and pricing strategy up front. In exchange for agreeing to buy at least 90 percent of its food products from Pate Dawson, the independent restaurateur receives Pate Dawson's buying expertise, which helps him or her substantially reduce overall food costs. Everyone wins: Pate Dawson earns a higher margin by delivering more products per delivery stop, while the restaurateur earns a higher margin by buying more efficiently.

As of 2005, Pate Dawson had a growth rate above the industry average. The firm had added more than a hundred jobs to the local economy in Goldsboro, North Carolina, over the past five years. Imagine Mac Sullivan's shock, then, to hear that Sysco, his largest competitor, was planning to build a distribution center twenty-five miles up the road in the city of Selma, and that the North Carolina and local governments would pay Sysco $10.2 million dollars in incentives to bring three to four hundred new jobs to the area.

Placing some calls, Sullivan learned that Sysco was set to receive a $5.2 million job development grant from the state of North Carolina based on the number of jobs the firm was adding. Sysco would also receive $2.2 million from the county government—$1.7 million in an economic development grant, and the rest in the form of a property-tax exemption spread over five years. The city of Selma, meanwhile, was kicking in $2.7 million: $1 million in the form of free electricity, another $1 million as a property-tax exemption, and the remainder in the form of exemption from water and sewer fees. As Sullivan notes, "$10.2 million doesn't sound like such a big deal, but consider this: With my industry's low margins, you need to bring in about $500 million in revenue to net $10.2 million in after-tax income. So, in effect, my state and local governments just handed my largest competitor a check representing half a billion dollars in business so that they could build a facility down the street from my firm. And, by the way, my firm has not only been steadily adding jobs; we've been part of the economy here for over a hundred years!"

To get some answers and voice his objections, Sullivan contacted his local government officials. The key person to speak with was the state of North Carolina's commerce secretary, who refused for weeks to return his call. Finally, in the fall of 2005, a meeting was scheduled. When Sullivan entered the room, he was surprised to find that a state lawyer had come to supervise what was supposed to have been a casual, friendly discussion. Unbowed, Sullivan sat down and explained that Sysco's promises to move three to four hundred jobs to the area was not what it seemed. "I told them that our industry only grows four to five percent a year. How in the world are they going to add three to four hundred jobs? What they're going to have to do is shift the majority of those jobs from other facilities within the state, or perhaps from facilities in other states. Either way, the net job growth will be much lower than it seems, if not zero. And here I am, adding a hundred new jobs—*real* jobs—based on my own innovations."

The attorney seemed dumbstruck by what he was hearing, yet the state secretary was unmoved. Sullivan asked the secretary: How had he evaluated Sysco's promises? Had he talked to anyone in the industry? As Sullivan relates, "He admitted that he hadn't; he'd relied on his department's own research. And they just don't have the specialized knowledge. But the secretary's mind was made up. I knew he wasn't going to listen." Shortly thereafter, it was announced that of the 345 workers Sysco planned to employ the first year, at least 165 would be brought in from existing facilities. That didn't stop Governor Mike Easley from proclaiming, in January 2005, that "Sysco's decision to locate in North Carolina is a tremendous win for the company, the community, and the state. They chose North Carolina because of our excellent workforce, our continuing support of education, and our business-friendly climate."[28]

Announcement of the Sysco deal occasioned loud criticism from citizens and groups opposed to government handouts to public corporations. Defending the state's economic incentives program, Democratic State Senator Walter Dalton remarked: "Any time you're creating jobs in distressed areas, that's a good thing. Everybody has questions about the incentives game played between states, but as long as other states can do it, we have to compete."[29] Suffice it to say that Mac Sullivan has a different perspective:

> I'm a guy who's innovating in an industry that's almost impossible to innovate. Sysco is not innovating—they're mainly leveraging their size to get ahead. So who is doing more for the economy? Look, unlike Sysco, I'm not asking for a handout. What I want is for government to do no harm. In terms of my business, I'm not worried about Sysco. Keep the playing field level, and we'll be fine. Yet we don't really have a level playing field these days.

The preceding chapters have sought to guide individual entrepreneurs as they navigate the dangerous territory of No Man's Land. To close the book, I'd like to step back and take a look at the important economic role played by growth firms. The entrepreneurs I've met don't always understand how critical their efforts are to our country's continued prosperity. By presenting evidence that growth firms are indeed a national treasure, I hope to affirm the value of entrepreneurialism and inspire these bold innovators to weather the hard road ahead. At the same time, my interactions with policy makers have revealed that they and the economists they rely upon also haven't sufficiently recognized growth firms' profound economic contributions. When politicians set out to favor small companies or large corporations, they sometimes enact legislation that burdens growth firms unnecessarily. Later in the chapter, I'll provide concrete suggestions for how government at all levels can better protect our entrepreneurial gems. First, though, let's examine some characteristics of growth firms and their functioning in the larger economy.

A PROFILE OF GROWTH FIRMS

The respected physicist and mathematician David Birch has single-handedly pioneered the statistical analysis of growth firms.[30] He defines them as companies with an average revenue growth of at least 20 percent over a four-year period. About 350,000 such firms exist among America's roughly 20 million firms at any given time. Most of these companies are small to mid-sized, with only 5 percent employing over one hundred people after their four-year growth spurt. As the case studies in this book have demonstrated, growth firms are found in all sectors of the economy—in food distribution and logistics, in restaurants and medical surveillance, as well as in software and other technology categories (although less than 10 percent are categorized as high-tech). Growth firms are also not all young companies; up to half of them have been in business for at least fifteen years before suddenly experiencing rapid growth. Finally, growth firms crop up in all areas of the country, even in the midwestern "rust belt," or in rural North Carolina, where Mac Sullivan's firm is located. Other companies researched for this book took root in locales as diverse as Pennsylvania, Arizona, New York, Maryland, and Colorado.[31]

Statistics on Growth Firms in the United States

- Average revenue growth of at least 20 percent over a 4-year period
- 350,000 at any given time
- Only 5 percent employing over 100 people
- Found in all industries and geographical areas

ENGINES OF THE ECONOMY

Growth firms represent a small portion of our nation's total population of firms—no more than a few percent, at most five. Why, then, are they so important? Two reasons: jobs and innovation.

As Birch's pathbreaking research has shown, large corporations and small mom-and-pop operations do not create most of our economy's jobs; emerging growth firms do. Between 1989 and 1993, growth firms—or "gazelles," as Birch calls them—added 4.4 million jobs at a time when the overall economy barely expanded at all. Between 1994 and 1998, gazelles went on to account for 95 percent of total job growth, adding 10.7 million out of 11.1 million new jobs created. Moreover, a small subset of "superstar" gazelles—those that began their growth with one hundred or more employees—created 61 percent of all gazelle job growth from 1994 to 1998. Explaining

gazelles' stunning job productivity, Birch points to smaller firms' ability to adapt to rapidly changing market conditions. "A fifty-person company can change direction quickly and a five-thousand-person company cannot," he has told me. "You have the ability and the resources to change, and you're not so big that your determination to change gets frustrated."[32]

Growth Firms: A National Treasure

Why do growth firms hire so many people? One reason is that these firms are in the process of systemizing or automating their businesses as they move to scale, and thus require more workers. Also, large companies enjoy access to capital, and frequently deploy it rather than human beings in situations where capital deployment is cheaper. Growth firms, by contrast, cannot deploy financial capital, since all too often they lack access to it.

Beyond adding jobs, growth firms are responsible for a disproportionate share of the economy's innovations—two-thirds, by one estimation.[33] The Nobel Prize–winning economist Edmund S. Phelps has written that "[a]lthough much innovation comes from established companies . . . much comes from start-ups, particularly the most novel innovations."[34] *The Economist* likewise has noted that market breakthroughs typically don't originate in corporate research and development departments, but rather in "scrappy new firms, twin-born with the invention itself." William Baumol, a distinguished Princeton and NYU economist and one of the world's foremost experts on entrepreneurship, explains this fact by observing that breakthrough thinking is the kind that only renegade entrepreneurs can accomplish, and that these entrepreneurs are also the only ones willing to take the extreme economic risks necessary to get their ideas off the ground.[35]

Powered by breakthrough ideas, gazelles shake up markets, exerting pressure on larger public companies to innovate. In this respect, they are far different from most small businesses. As an academic report quoted earlier explained, "not all businesses are dynamic and entrepreneurial ventures—introducing new ideas/methods/solutions to the production of goods and services in a market economy."[36] In sum, growth firms are uniquely able to introduce new ideas to the market quickly and efficiently. When acquired by larger firms, they come to serve as corporate America's de facto research and development arm.

Growth firms are becoming an increasingly important market for large American firms. As Sherri Leopard, CEO of Leopard, part of the Ogilvy family of companies and one of the nation's leading experts on marketing to small and mid-sized businesses (SMB), notes, large firms who want to grow have no choice but to appeal to gazelles. Given the economy's speed of change, any services firm that wants to obtain and keep a meaningful share of the Fortune 2000 as customers in the future must catch gazelles early on, since many will appear on the Fortune 2000 list in seven to ten years. "A lot of large firms used to target large transactions and live off them for years. To grow in today's world, you have to be nimble enough to service clients of all sizes—especially gazelles, the most important part of the SMB market."

THE HISTORICAL CONTEXT*

By driving innovation, growth firms play an even larger macroeconomic role in that they help to ensure America's continued competitiveness. As one well-known executive coach reminds us, "the lifeblood of every person, company, and even the country's success is innovation

---

*I had the privilege of interviewing Drs. Baumol and Birch together in a free-ranging conversation. Dr. Baumol's comments about the convergence of entrepreneurs and money, along with his comment that private equity showed up on the scene in the early eighties because of legislation that allowed pension plans to invest in equity, provoked Dr. Birch to remark that he began to see the emergence of gazelles as a force in the economy at about the same time. I will leave it to researchers to delve into the significance of this relationship.

and the creation of new opportunity."[37] By one estimate, growth firms account for a full two-thirds of the differences in economic growth rates among industrialized nations.[38]

Now, why is this? Professor Birch understands growth firms' economic significance as a fairly recent development brought about by broad structural changes—specifically, the industrial economy's decline at the hands of the knowledge economy. As he points out, the mid- to late-1980s represents an important inflection point when innovation started driving growth to a far greater extent than it had. Fortune 500 firms as a group began to shed jobs starting in 1979, whereas for some twenty-five years previously they had added jobs year after year. It is curious, I think, that the 1980s was exactly the period that saw the beginning of private equity's exponential growth.

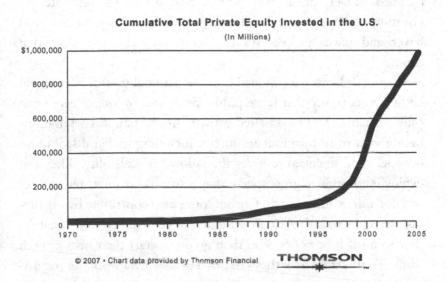

Cumulative Total Private Equity Invested in the U.S.
(In Millions)

© 2007 · Chart data provided by Thomson Financial   THOMSON

Birch notes a number of other, accompanying social trends, such as the emergence of women as entrepreneurs and the decrease in the length of product life cycles.[39] Relating the latter to growth firms, Birch observes that "during a time when technology is changing very fast and a new global market opens up almost every month, younger firms are more able to start fresh without all the baggage of the past and seize new opportunities quickly."[40]

Professor Baumol also sees novelty in the economic power of entrepreneurialism, although he puts the critical inflection point much earlier—at the end of the Middle Ages. Before that time, he argues, the entrepreneurial spirit was alive and well, but military pursuits then determined the allocation of wealth, so that was where all the entrepreneurial energy went. In the centuries since, entrepreneurs have tended to "follow the money" and apply their ingenuity to commercially relevant projects such as bridges or steam engines. Like Birch, however, Baumol judges innovation—and the rapid-growth firms that pursue it—as pivotal to America's economic growth going forward. "There is no way we are going to get out of the innovation business. In fact, the one way *not* to survive is to fail to innovate. Innovation is all we've got. Productivity is rising quickly, so you need fewer and fewer people. It's the innovation and the ideas that count."[41]

If growth firms have indeed become national treasures, it would be incorrect to say that large public firms are no longer economically valuable. Unlike smaller growth firms, public corporations have access to tremendous resources, including global distribution networks and financial reserves that allow for scalability. They can deploy innovation at great speed; they just can't create it, and as a result don't drive job growth. Corporations also contribute by nurturing managers who then break off and lead growth firms. Alternately, they spin off innovators, who then go on to start their own growth firms. To illustrate how these last two phenomena work, let me unravel a family tree of sorts that has grown out of a single corporation, Texas Instruments.

As Harold Blomquist, CEO of the microchip company Simtek, has related to me, a man by the name of Dr. Richard Petritz started working at Texas Instruments, then left and helped found a highly successful tech start-up known as Mostek.[42] Out of that firm, another one, Inmos, formed in 1978. By 1984, Inmos became a $150 million company and was funded by the British government. Then Inmos was privatized and handed off to different companies. Petritz left at this time to start a third technology firm, Simtek. Blomquist became a member of the board, and when Petritz died in 2003, he became chairman.

As Blomquist notes, Texas Instruments and Inmos nurtured a number of talented people who then went on to build growth firms:

> A bunch of technology guys left Texas Instruments when Inmos was formed, followed by another group of marketing, sales, public relations, and business development folks. Paul Schroeder, founder of Inmos, left following its sale to form Maximum Storage and a number of follow-up enterprises, including Anchor-Chip Technologies. Doug Rankin, senior vice president of sales and marketing at Inmos, went on to Signetics and then Actel, the latter of which is now a very successful and well-established company. Ron Sartore, one of the real smart guys that left my group, had developed a number of industry standard products at Texas Instruments, and went on to become a serial entrepreneur. There is a whole network of us that have gone on to lead and be a part of many successful endeavors.

Reflecting on his career, Blomquist notes that the bigger companies get, the more ideas they generate, but the more reluctant they also become to implement those ideas. As a result, "there's a spinning out of people who can't push their ideas through the corporate morass." Looking back on it, Blomquist considers Texas Instruments "like the Stanford Training Institute." The firm, he notes, spun out literally thousands of engineers and business managers—professionals who cut their teeth on an industry leader, then applied their skills elsewhere.

Economic growth thus depends not on growth firms' economic dominance at the expense of corporations, but on a flourishing *partnership* between the two. As Baumol notes, "You need both gazelles and big companies. Intel didn't invent chips or the computer, but it has been making incremental improvements, improving clock-speed by five million percent over thirty years. You need the David and Goliath partnership. The Davids get the breakthroughs, and the Goliaths apply their resources to institutionalize those breakthroughs as only they can."[43]

SHOOTING OURSELVES IN THE FOOT

If growth firms contribute so much to our prosperity, why do state and local governments incentivize public corporations, thus tipping the playing field soundly in their favor? The answer is surprising. After testifying before Congress, meeting with representatives of the Federal Reserve, and having discussions with policy makers at all levels, I've concluded that many people in power are simply unaware of growth firms' profound economic role. Moreover, I've discovered that the discipline of economics, whose teachings shape and inform policy making in this country, has not only virtually nothing to say about growth firms, but has ignored the profound differences between growth firms and small companies. Only now, in fact, is this beginning to change. In a paper presented at the 2006 meetings of the American Economic Association, the prominent economist Carl J. Schramm wrote:

> Despite being overlooked or explicitly written out of our economic drama, it turns out that entrepreneurs are resilient in ways never appreciated. Indeed, we are now coming to understand that they have an evergreen role to play. They appear to be the sustaining force of democratic capitalism. Thus, in addition to being a species that is apparently hard to see and difficult to exterminate, they play a central role in the undisputed objective of our managed economy, namely, growth.[44]

In effect, neither economic policy nor theory has caught up with the broader structural changes in the economy recognized by Birch and Baumol. Lacking an understanding of entrepreneurialism, we simply don't run the economy today in the interests of growth firms. As a result, our misguided policies needlessly injure growth firms, preventing the economy from reaching its true potential.

Before government can become truly mindful of growth firms' needs, economists must refine the paradigm of the "new economy" and develop a new arsenal of tools to measure it. I'm involved with starting a nonprofit organization in collaboration with Professor Birch that we hope will contribute to this effort by creating a new economic index related to entrepreneurialism. Called the "No Man's Land Index," this tool will measure the number of firms that achieve "escape velocity" and successfully navigate through No Man's Land. Our hope is that this tool will increase politicians' sensitivity to the needs of growth firms, giving them the economic rationale they need to avoid policies—such as incentives to public corporations—that irrationally tip the playing field against growth firms.

The direct subsidization of public corporations is hardly the only policy-based challenge facing growth firms today. Lacking an appreciation of entrepreneurialism, politicians pass legislation that unwittingly places unnecessary burdens on promising young firms that are already struggling with the difficulties of No Man's Land. In the past, for instance, growth firms seeking experienced managers yet lacking the capital to offer competitive compensation could dispense stock options quickly and without undue hassle. Today regulations require that firms offering stock options undertake the expense of revaluing the firm every year. The net result is that stock options are increasingly not a viable option for many entrepreneurs. Those that still wish to draw top talent are struggling to find equally attractive compensation alternatives.

The extent to which restrictions on stock options matter to growth firms was brought home to me a few years back when I advised a brilliant French scientist on his new entrepreneurial venture and entrance into the private equity world. Meeting with this gentleman in Paris, I tackled the obvious questions: Where should he locate his business?

Whom should he hire? How should he compensate them? When we explored the inclusion of stock options, we were shocked to find that there was no way, given French law and despite the use of world-class attorneys and accountants, to get stock options to the employees of a French start-up without incurring huge tax consequences. I'll never forget what it was like to lounge around in an absolutely stunning villa in the south of France, in the aftermath of a sensational meal, talking about how this innovative start-up might have to move its employees to America for the sole purpose of getting them stock.

Today I fear that America is rapidly moving in the direction of France, becoming a place where growth firms find it nearly impossible to do business. The chart below compares French policy concerning stock options circa 2000 with American policy at that time and now. As you can see, we have already made it significantly more difficult for growth firms to attract the talent they need to get up and running and grow through No Man's Land. Unless politicians begin to consider the effects of accounting and tax policy on growth firms, the situation will only get worse, and all of us will lose. Remember: Less talent for growth firms means more business failures, fewer jobs, less innovation, and, ultimately, lower economic growth.

ANALYSIS OF STOCK OPTION COMPLEXITIES

United States 2000	United States Now	France 2000
No: Valuation requirements	**Yes:** Valuation requirements	**Yes:** Valuation requirements
No: Special accounting treatment	**Yes:** Special accounting treatment	**Yes:** Special accounting treatment
No: "Qualified options" are not taxable to an individual upon exercise.	**Yes:** "Qualified options" could be taxable to an individual upon exercise.	**No:** "Qualified options" are not taxable to an individual upon exercise.

No: The company is not directly taxed on the employees' gain upon exercise of "nonqualified options."	**No:** The company is not directly taxed on the employees' gain upon exercise of "nonqualified options."	**Yes:** The company is directly taxed on the employees' gain upon exercise of "nonqualified options."

If growth firms in America are having a more difficult time attracting talent, they are also experiencing needless hardships when it comes to raising the capital required to complete the transition out of No Man's Land. Traditionally, the initial public offering represented a substantially cheaper means of generating capital than a private equity sale, making it the financial tool of choice for many entrepreneurs exiting No Man's Land. Thanks to compliance measures mandated by Sarbanes-Oxley, however, this is no longer true. Using information I received from a firm that specializes in valuations and that has experience with both public and private companies, I estimate that equity capital for a small public firm costs 18 to 22 percent of the capital raised, depending on the degree of risk. Yet this figure does not include the estimated $1 million to $3 million it costs to comply with Sarbanes-Oxley provisions. Assuming a $2 million yearly marginal cost of compliance on a $30 million to $40 million public offering, the real cost of public capital for entrepreneurs stands at 23 to 29 percent of the amount raised, making public equity the more costly option. By rendering financing more expensive, economic policy has unwittingly made the task of emerging from No Man's Land that much more difficult for an innovative, job-producing growth firm.

DO NO HARM

Mac Sullivan is right: Growth firms don't enjoy a level playing field these days. A more enlightened economic policy, I believe, would be based in large part on the Hippocratic oath's concept of "Do no harm." With a few small exceptions, activist approaches to fostering entrepreneurship are impracticable, and even wind up doing more harm than good. As Professor Birch's work with the Swedish government has shown, public officials are invariably worse than the equity markets themselves in picking entrepreneurial winners.[45] More to the point, handouts to entrepreneurs are unnecessary. Unlike public corporations, the entrepreneurs I've spoken with aren't asking for government handouts. All they want is for government to get out of the way and let the market do the work of sorting out good innovations from bad.

One thing government can do, beyond rolling back incentives to public corporations and revising accounting and tax policies that threaten growth firms, is to limit the administrative impediments to innovation. "In Australia," Professor Baumol notes, "it takes three days to get a business started, while in some Latin American countries it takes a year and a half. By cutting out the red tape, Australia has gone a long way toward making itself hospitable to entrepreneurial ventures." Likewise, Baumol would do away with welfare state–style restrictions on hiring and firing. "In Europe, high unemployment is partly explained by the fact that you can't fire people easily after they've been working at a job for three months. Such laws are frequently passed with good intentions, but they impede a growth firm's ability to adapt to market conditions."[46]

As far as positive policy measures go, Baumol advocates that government play a far greater role in funding the basic scientific research that leads, ultimately, to marketable innovations and the creation of growth firms. "If the next president of the United States was sitting here in front of me," Baumol says, "I'd tell him or her to put money into the National Science Foundation, which has been cut back for years."

Adjustments in tax policy comprise an even more promising means by which government can support entrepreneurship without resorting to handouts or otherwise subverting the free market's efficient operation. In 2001, a piece of legislation I designed—H.R. 3062, also called the BRIDGE Act—received strong bipartisan support before finally dying in committee.[47] The bill would have allowed a growth firm to defer up to $250,000 in federal income tax liability for two years, with payment over a four-year period. If the bill had passed, it would have helped entrepreneurs deal with the potentially deadly money issues that crop up in No Man's Land, without costing the government revenue. In fact, by Congressional Joint Tax Committee staff calculations, the BRIDGE act would have resulted in temporary revenue "losses" over the first four years, but a $1.1 billion revenue *gain* over ten years, since entrepreneurs would have been required to pay the deferred taxes with interest once the dangers of No Man's Land had passed.

As we saw in chapter 5, many businesses fail simply because they cannot maneuver through the capital gap and secure the $250,000 to $1 million they need beyond what the entrepreneur's personal credit will allow. By permitting these firms to defer taxes, the BRIDGE Act would have reduced the need for capital during the No Man's Land transition, thus making it possible for firms to grow to the point where they could more readily attract a $1 million or more credit line. In addition, cash temporarily freed up by the BRIDGE Act would have allowed entrepreneurs to better weather the cash-flow problems firms encounter as they ramp up for rapid growth.

Patrick Von Bargen, executive director of the National Commission on Entrepreneurialism, called the BRIDGE Act "a workable, creative, win-win idea." Kate O'Beirne, Washington editor of the *National Review*, wrote that the BRIDGE Act was "the most elegant way to help the most promising entrepreneurs."[48] *Inc.* magazine's former editor-in-chief George Gendron wrote: "The BRIDGE Act is an ingenious, fiscally sound mechanism for keeping billions in the hands of a group that makes the most efficient use of capital."[49] Although the measure didn't pass, I remain hopeful that it will pass in the future with the support of leaders as diverse as Senator John

Kerry, Senator Olympia Snowe, Representative Jim DeMint, Representative Brian Baird, and others.

THE FINAL PAUSE POINT

In an interview appearing in *Investor's Business Daily,* Home Depot founder Bernie Marcus recounts being asked if he could have built the company if he had had to conform to today's laws and accounting regulations. "I honestly don't believe we could," Marcus responds.

> We went public after opening our fourth store because we needed the capital to open more stores. Going public and entrepreneurship were the keys to our success. If you're a public company today, you have to be surrounded with lawyers on the one side of you and an accountant on the other side. Today, you just can't use your business judgment to take the risks that must be taken for a new company to succeed.[50]

Marcus's comments should serve as a wake-up call to policy makers reading this book. Growth firms are in fact a national treasure, and unless something is done, their future prospects are in jeopardy.

Previous pause points in this book have served as opportunities for entrepreneurs to stand back and examine their businesses from a new perspective. In this final pause point, I hope that policy makers will take a moment to reexamine their own assumptions about today's economy and how best to grow it. Do incentives for established corporations really contribute to the overall economic vitality of your jurisdiction? When it comes to businesses that create jobs for your constituents, might it not work better to foster emerging growth firms in your own backyard?

I also hope that entrepreneurs will take a moment to reflect once more upon their businesses, this time with a sense of measured optimism. However grim Marcus's comments seem, they should not be taken to imply that entrepreneurialism has been entirely thwarted, nor that it is now impossible for determined entrepreneurs to grow through No Man's Land. As we've seen over and over again in this book, entrepreneurs *do* succeed with growth firms, as long as they do two things: take the time to think strategically about their business, and work conscientiously to apply the fundamental navigational rules. If the day-to-day challenges of growth are getting the better of you, I invite you to flip back through these pages and remind yourself of firms like Noodles & Company, Investors Mortgage Holdings, Chamberlin Edmonds, and George's Music. In their unique ways, each of these companies has weathered growth's inevitable challenges and the sometimes forbidding competitive environment to become a leader in its respective category. If you adhere to the four *M*s, and if growth suits your personal tastes and financial interests, then with steadfastness and hard work your firm can transition through No Man's Land, reach escape velocity, and grow to the success that lies beyond.

Ultimately, I hope entrepreneurs will come away from this book taking heart, and also taking pride. Taking heart, because with this book in hand you now have the tools and the knowledge to wrest back control of a growth business and make it the best it can possibly be—however *you* define that. Taking pride, too, because despite the odds, you've already accomplished so much. Unlike most people in our economy, you had the guts to break with convention, take your chances, and follow your dream. Whether you win or lose, your drive and determination to innovate has in some small measure already helped to create prosperity for us all. You have done something special—something to make the world a better place—and to me, that's worth celebrating.

Gazelles and Corporate R&D

Excerpted from my article "Innovating the Development
of Innovation: Gazelles and Corporate R&D"
Research-Technology Management (May 2007)

Overview: Disruptive innovations increasingly originate in private-
sector emerging growth firms—or gazelles, as they're commonly called.
Unfortunately, corporate managers find it difficult to replicate the
unique ecosystem that spawns the rapid innovation driven by these
companies. This white paper discusses the reasons for these difficulties
and suggests how a large corporation might use the gazelle ecosystem—
including the private equity sponsors that invest in it—to speed delivery
of the corporation's own internal R&D ideas.

Gazelles and the Innovation Ecosystem

Gazelles deliver innovation because they exist in a unique ecosystem
that is virtually impossible to replicate in a large corporate environment. Recognizing this uniqueness is key to understanding why a
large corporation might wish to seed its own innovations into
gazelles. Gazelles and established corporations differ primarily in
their approach to the market, management culture, business model,
and financial needs.

Approach to the Market: Corporations prepare extensively in advance of a product launch. They conduct market research, develop a clear understanding of the target customer, and develop strategies for how to minimize risk and ensure that product demand is large enough to justify the money invested in the launch. Gazelles, by contrast, typically don't understand who the ultimate customer is while developing and launching a product. They improvise as they go, making opportunistic promises to customers that in turn change the product and the company. Their business is a living laboratory, a process of *discovering* what ultimately is the right product, service, and target customer. Early customers lead the gazelle to other customers, and the promises made to these new customers rarely size up with the existing delivery capabilities of the gazelle. Much of the innovation, then, occurs during the process of meeting the challenges of the promises made.

This process is anathema to the proven discipline of a larger organization. It contradicts every assumption about a larger company's plan for launch, including the larger firm's selection of a distribution channel. In the early stages, the gazelle's innovation process requires proximity to the customer base that many times precludes the use of the existing distribution channel available to the large corporation. In fact, a gazellelike approach to introducing a new corporate innovation might initially require a separate or a totally different channel than the one used for sales and distribution of the corporation's core products or services. In most cases, gazelles and major corporations also execute diametrically opposite cultural approaches to introducing an idea into the market. The corporation is correctly looking to create a widget to plug into their distribution engines so as to create immediate economic leverage, while the gazelle just wants to create a widget that is an innovation for the customers before them at the time. The gazelle innovates because it is perfectly situated to listen to the market and make promises to customers that require innovation borne out of necessity.

The Management Culture: In the corporate world, most managers are rewarded and measured according to revenues and earnings they drive. Among gazelles, by contrast, management is rewarded and measured on the basis of value created, without this value in the formative early stages being expressed directly in revenue or profit. Gazelles innovate product, processes, and distribution channels. These innovations can be directly valued by professional private equity investors, who recognize the important chess moves that are made in advance of launching a business into its ultimate economic leverage. As private equity understands, the appropriate focus at the inception of an emerging-growth enterprise might be on product design over profitability, since many times gazelles must meet a series of customer needs with little thought as to the economic consequences. To be sure, those decisions must be based on the expectations that investments will ultimately lead to earnings. However, the leadership of a gazelle is instinctively oriented around the development of value through innovation, not the ultimate value of economic leverage (i.e., driving earnings through process efficiencies at large-volume revenue). Thus the measurement and reward culture of a large corporation diverges from the gazelle's. Tensions emerge when corporate managers responsible for launching a new idea encounter value-creation opportunities that they instinctively know should be pursued even when there is no proven or logical road ahead to economic leverage. Economic leverage ultimately has to be introduced into the equation, but usually after certain elements of value have been created and the business and its targeted customers are defined.

To compound the cultural issues, the gazelle's leadership needs to change dramatically and rapidly in accordance with the stages of growth through which the gazelle is passing. The production management or product development skills needed to keep the firm's operations aligned with an ever-changing set of customer promises in the early stages of a new product's development are quite different from the skills and expertise needed to drive the business into economic scale. This rapid turnover is often difficult for a larger firm to accept or manage.

The Business Model: When large firms invest in new ideas, they typically do so in hopes of plugging those ideas into the corporation's existing business model and leveraging its existing scale. One of the key experiments that go on in an emerging growth business is the discovery of a value proposition—the key differentiator, the real sustainable and scalable innovation. In other words, new sustainable competitive advantage and the operating leverage that drives profits with sales volume is the ultimate test of the corporation's development of innovation. In my experience, creation of a differentiated value proposition powerful enough to disrupt a market and the scaling of this proposition rarely happen simultaneously. One (innovation) comes before the other (economic scale), and an emerging business typically can't muster the expertise and the bandwidth to discover both simultaneously, let alone execute it simultaneously. The scalability issue is actually twofold; i.e., how does the gazelle as a business itself scale, and how does it scale within the corporate mother ship. At its best, a gazelle works to build its own operating leverage. Adding the additional simultaneous burden of creating its own scale based on predetermined assumptions that the mother ship should be leveraged can be fatal.

In summary, the old adage that the whole (the new idea and the existing corporate enterprise) is greater than the sum of its parts has almost always been based on leveraging the larger corporate business model. I contend that actually executing that idea on behalf of the large corporation could best be done by allowing an idea to foster in the gazelle ecosystem until it has found its own scale before an attempt is made to integrate it into the larger corporate enterprise.

The Money: Corporate capital deployment cycles are usually annual or at least no more frequent than quarterly. Gazelles, by contrast, require *quick, opportunistic* infusions of cash. This is why private equity firms don't give gazelles extensive capital up front, but are quick to give it when an opportunity presents itself. No one in management likes to operate on a cliff's edge, but the simple reality is that this is where innovation occurs. Opportunistic processes require opportunistic capital.

Judgments on capital deployment can diverge considerably from the traditional methods of deploying capital within a large corporation. For example, a gazelle might deploy capital to create a final service or product that delivers an amazing value proposition to a client even though the gazelle lacks a clear understanding of how that product might ultimately be distributed or how it will scale. The early distribution approach for that product might include the creation of a channel that conflicts with those favored by the corporation. The management team of a gazelle might have created a sensational new idea for the customer well before figuring out how to turn it into profits at large volumes. Funding such ideas is completely logical within the gazelle enterprise but becomes completely illogical when vetted in capital budgeting terms from a corporate perspective.

Strategic Implications

The barriers to successfully replicating the innovation environment of the gazelle ecosystem in a large corporation are extreme, so much so that I am suggesting that corporations consider deploying an intermediary into their development equation to take advantage of the ecosystem. Attempts to change the ground rules or the ecosystems that have proven so successful for gazelles or for large corporations will almost certainly not work.

The key is to insert professional private equity investors and their existing portfolio companies into the R&D product-launch equation with a set of institutionalized, predetermined rules that corporations and private equity investors can use to meet their mutual objectives.

The private equity environment in the United States today is ripe for linking private equity sponsors and the gazelles that they have invested in with the R&D process of large corporate America. After all, it is major public corporations that end up facing innovation from these gazelles in the marketplace and, in many cases, ultimately purchasing them. Many of these companies have already been sponsored by private equity.

Large corporations maintain investments in R&D innovations that could matter tremendously to the existing portfolio company investments of private equity sponsors. Corporations currently have management teams charged with developing and integrating those ideas into long-term sustainable businesses. These innovations could be provided (loaned, if you will) to existing private equity portfolio companies in exchange for predetermined rights to purchase those companies back at multiples that meet the private equity return thresholds. Existing private equity portfolio firms that operate in the markets near and dear to the corporation could use those innovations developed within corporate R&D departments, as well as the customer relationships owned by corporations, to drive market innovation. Many of these portfolio companies have distribution channels and pockets of potential new customers for large corporations; the addition of innovation provided out of corporate R&D could supercharge the ability of portfolio companies to mature a set of ideas into a scalable business. These collaborations could provide unique opportunities for large companies to test the market viability of emerging ideas at lightning speed by launching them into an existing platform: gazelles sponsored by private equity. Under predetermined rules (the right to purchase the company back under a fixed multiple of cash flow after a predetermined period), they then can bring these emerging ideas back into the corporate fold when they are truly ready and able to be integrated.

In today's environment, cooperative relationships with private equity sponsors opens the way to increased speed to market, lower risk of failure, and increased chances of integrating innovation into a large corporation's earnings stream. A large corporation has an opportunity to replicate the optimal conditions for developing innovation in a market by placing its ideas in existing gazelles far enough along in their development to be sponsored with professional private equity backing. Although I am not directly aware of any private equity firms that have negotiated a deal as I have proposed above, a number of private equity sponsors that specialize in the middle market have confirmed directly with me in recent conversations a willingness to provide major corporate contributors of R&D the right to purchase portfolio companies back at a predetermined multiple. The interesting question is whether a large corporation would hand over an idea developed in the corporate R&D department completely to a gazelle and its private equity backer. Given the explanation of the unique ecosystem that spawns innovation, it's possible that some of the outstanding innovation developed in corporate America has a better chance of commercialization if grafted into an existing innovator supported by private equity investors skilled at understanding and supporting the gazelle ecosystem.

APPENDIX II

Further Discussion of Private Equity

Preferred Stock and the Prater Case

In chapter 7, Burt Prater faced a critical choice: either take on more private equity to support an outsourcing opportunity, or realign his core business with the market and position the company for sale. A critical factor in this decision was Burt's realization that the common shareholders would not make more money if the business took on the new outsourcing business, even though the business would be much bigger and could sell for a greater multiple. This state of affairs owed to the liquidation preferences rights that the private equity firm had negotiated as part of its equity investment. So how do the rights held by private equity firms actually work in a real deal under real circumstances? How do private equity investors think about the companies in which they invest? These are critical questions for readers thinking of taking on outside equity capital.*

---

*For more information about deal structuring for company investment and acquisitions, consider Clinton Richardson's *Growth Company Guide 4.0—Investors, Deal Structures and Legal Strategies*, to be published in September 2007. The prior edition, *Growth Company Guide 2000*, by the same author, may also be useful and is available online at growco.com.

Toward a Private Equity Investor's Perspective

Imagine that a good friend of yours has told you that a woman he knows has a business that's growing, has great potential, and needs an outside equity investor. The amount she is asking for is significant—$3.5 million. You have done well in your own business, but that amount of money is out of the question—unless you round up a number of your friends who trust your business instincts and who, like you, are prepared to invest.

You meet the woman who started the business and are immediately convinced of the business's potential. You know a lot about the business's market, and you think that she is on the right track. So you decide to do the deal. You contact a number of your friends, and they agree to pool their money and invest along with you, as long as you agree to monitor the company and serve on its board of directors. Your friends propose that you receive 2 percent of the total investment, or seventy thousand dollars, to be paid annually by the investors on a prorated basis, and 20 percent of all the profits that the group makes above 8 percent per year compounded. This compensation is meant to rally your focus and help assure that the company maximizes its potential with the capital.

You are good to go. Yet several days before the closing you run into an old friend and business associate—we'll call him Maxwell—whom you tell about the deal. Looking you squarely in the eye, Max insists that the two of you go to lunch before the closing of your investment the following week. There Max tells you of an investment situation that he was recently involved with—different company, different industry, but the same basic arrangement as the one you are pursuing, i.e., an individual (Max) investing a whole lot of money on behalf of his buddies. As Max reveals, things didn't work out as he had planned. The problem did not involve the business, but rather a gradual and complete misunderstanding that had developed between him (the investor) and the entrepreneur concerning investment objectives. Several situations arose that Max felt had hugely affected the investment he had made on behalf of his friends.

There was a short period when the company needed additional capital to continue growing, and Max was in a position to come up with more money. The capital was going to be put to good use, and he believed in the business. The problem was that the entrepreneur grew wary of taking too much money from a single investor (apparently one of his friends had told him that it was not a good idea) and decided to take on capital from another individual. This individual got to buy in at a slightly lower price than the price Max had paid almost eighteen months earlier. In other words, Max was significantly diluted in his ownership of the company and received no value for the capital that had helped the company grow for eighteen months. There was nothing Max could do about it, because he did not have a majority of the shares or a majority of the seats on the board of directors. The entrepreneur really wanted the new investor on the board. The new investor insisted on a price slightly lower than the original price, and he prevailed.

It has now been more than five years since Max invested money into the company. The company was doing well, and in fact there had been a number of large companies interested in acquiring it. Yet the original entrepreneur had no interest in selling. His salary and bonus had increased threefold over the last five years, and although there was evidence in the marketplace that the company might best be positioned for growth within a larger organization, the entrepreneur liked what he was doing and had little inclination to sell. To his credit, he also felt that he could keep the company growing, and that ultimately it would be worth even more money to the investors. When Max raised concerns about turning down offers to buy the company, the entrepreneur responded that he did not understand "what the big rush" was. To make matters worse, Max indicated that his buddies, the ones who had trusted him to invest in the company in the first place, were getting antsy. When would they get their money back, and a cash return? It was great to know that the stock was obviously worth more than they paid for it, but that didn't do them any good; there was no market for the shares of this privately held company. They wanted cash. Some of Max's buddies really needed the money for personal reasons, and the pressure on him was becoming unbearable. They couldn't understand why Max couldn't convince the entrepreneur to sell the company so that everyone would walk away a winner.

After hearing Max's story you leave your lunch date with a huge pit in your stomach. You're thinking about these and related scenarios. You hadn't considered that the business might need even *more* capital, nor had you ever thought about how a decision to sell the company might be decided. To be honest, you hadn't conceived of the fact that maybe things wouldn't work out and the company would be sold for less than you had invested in it.

Private Equity Investment Scenarios and Safeguards

Who is the bad guy in the above story? In my opinion, no one. Those involved simply maintain completely different sets of expectations that have not been worked through prior to the investment. When individuals are investing their friends' money and they begin to play out such scenarios in their head, they begin to take on the private equity investor's perspective. What I'd like to do now is walk you through some of the techniques that private equity investors have developed over the years to handle the situations described above. My purpose in doing this is to help readers pause and understand what taking on private equity will ultimately entail. What I have to say will no doubt discourage some readers from considering private equity. Yet it will help others understand the negotiations objectively and unemotionally and prepare them to take on professional investors as a constituency for whom they are now responsible.

Scenario 1: A new investor invests at a lower price

Most preferred stock owned by private equity investors has what is called an *antidilution right*. This allows the private equity investor to receive additional shares if new capital is taken in at a lower price, adjusting the investment retroactively so as to get the private equity investor the lower price, too. Some of these provisions include a right for the private equity investor to purchase additional shares even if the price is higher so that he can continue to maintain the same percentage of ownership. In the Prater case, the investor had the right to maintain his ownership of 39 percent at the lower valuation by receiving new shares at no cost if Burt decided to bring in an investor at a lower valuation than he invested in originally. The investor also retained the right to buy enough shares to maintain his ownership at 39 percent from a new offering if a new investor was brought in at a higher price.

Scenario 2: Investors wish to cash out before the entrepreneur does

Many preferred stock investment documents entitle the company to repurchase the investor's stock after a set period of time, say five years, at a fixed return. This is intended to provide the investor with needed liquidity but can force the company to come up with substantial cash at an inconvenient time. Other common provisions entitle the investor to force the management shareholders to sell their stock along with the investor if the investor has a purchase offer it finds acceptable. This removes management's flexibility to determine the best time to sell. These provisions are typically carefully negotiated.

Scenario 3: Investor liquidation preferences for management to think like the investor

Most preferred stock vehicles have a right referred to as a *liquidation preference* that really serves several purposes. First, it establishes a guaranteed return on the investment no matter what the price of the shares ultimately sell for. For example, the guaranteed return to the private equity investors in the Prater case was 8 percent annually on the original $3.5 million invested in the company, plus their 39 percent of any proceeds received above their original investment and an 8 percent compounded return, unless the company achieved a predetermined valuation, at which point the investors received only their 39 percent of the proceeds received for the company. Take a look at the schedule below; the longer the company waits before it sells and returns cash to the investors, the more the investors receive out of the ultimate proceeds.

% of Proceeds Received by Investors If the Valuation of the Company *Reaches* the Agreed-Upon Threshold of at Least 3X the Value at the Time of Investment	% of Proceeds Received by Investors If the Valuation of the Company *Does Not Reach* the Agreed-Upon Threshold at the Time of Investment
39% based on an exit in 4 years from the time of the investment—the value at the time of exit was calculated at **3X** the valuation at the time of the investment	**58%** based on an exit in 4 years from the time of the investment—the value at the time of exit was calculated at **2X** the valuation at the time of the investment
FINANCIAL OVERVIEW	FINANCIAL OVERVIEW
Original Valuation: **$9 million** Sales Price (3X): **$27 million**	Original Valuation: **$9 million** Sales Price (2X): **$18 million**
Common Shareholders— entrepreneur's and employees' share of proceeds: **$16.4 million**	Common Shareholders— entrepreneur's and employees' share of proceeds: **$7.5 million**
Preferred Stock—private equity investors' share of proceeds: **$10.6 million**	Preferred Stock—private equity investors' share of proceeds: **$10.5 million**
39% of the proceeds were received by the investors, i.e., their proportional	**58% even though they own 39% of the stock because the company's value**

| ownership because the company's value did reach the 3X valuation threshold | did not reach the 3X valuation threshold |

Note the huge difference between the percentage of proceeds received if the company reaches the agreed-upon threshold as opposed to if it doesn't. This elucidates the reasoning behind Burt's choice to position and sell the company. He could take on more money, but unless he drove value very quickly, most of the money would go to the investors. Burt was not in a position to run the company indefinitely; this type of preference takes the investor's urgent desire to turn the investment into cash and lays it on the shoulders of the entrepreneur and the leadership team. In other words, Burt couldn't respond by asking, "What's the big rush?" Burt embraced the investor's desire to turn the investment into cash in a reasonable period of time because he had to constantly add value ahead of the guaranteed 8 percent return embedded in the $3.5 million investment, and he needed to reach a minimum agreed-upon threshold.

The liquidation preference also deals with the opposite issue of the entrepreneur's premature sale of the company. If Burt had decided to sell the company at a lower valuation than what the investors had originally invested, they would have received their money back and an 8 percent return before Burt or any of the management of the company had received any proceeds.

Is this arrangement unfair to entrepreneurs? No. What *is* unfair is for you or any other entrepreneur to jump into the private equity world without recognizing that you now have to incorporate an investor's perspective into your own company. I suspect that if you as an entrepreneur were to start investing in other growth companies, you would very quickly find yourself negotiating the same types of rights for your investments.

So what does taking on an investor's perspective mean for entrepreneurs and the firms they've created? It forces entrepreneurs to become radically objective about their business, their management, and their measurements. This is a good thing. Remember, your personal net worth is most probably tied up in the company. Applying a true investor's perspective to the business forces it to make the tough changes necessary for continued growth. Note that an investor's perspective is not a short-term perspective. In fact, a recent article published in the *Financial Times* attributes the positive performance of family-controlled public companies precisely to their ability to shun short-term thinking.[51]

Taking on an investor's perspective changes the firm's culture. Remember, I defined culture in terms of a company's decision-making process. The culture will change because you have a new constituency involved in the decision-making process: an investor who needs to exit his or her investment in a timely fashion. Strategy—the new promises made to customers that will drive growth and profits—and the execution process required to maintain market alignment become focused on positioning the company to best maximize its long-term value. Burt Prater very shrewdly knew that positioning his company as a product for a larger company would likely drive more value more quickly for everyone, including the management team and the investors, than would taking on even more capital on the chance of growing an even larger business. He was right. Shortly after his realignment of the business as the low-cost provider of surveillance exams, his firm was sold to a larger company with multiple product offerings in the health-care market.

Conclusion

I have laid out only two of the scenarios that could play out in a company following the introduction of private equity capital. These scenarios are so vexing that many private equity firms will invest only if they maintain control over the company. Other private equity investors do invest as minority investors, but negotiate various rights with their stock (this is why their stock is referred to as preferred stock) to protect their investment. In no way have I meant for this appendix to scare you away from taking on professional private equity, public equity (going public), or any other kind of investor. I do hope that it helps you in your decision-making process. There are many businesses that can survive and grow quite nicely without rushing into the investment world. No one should proceed under any circumstances without thinking carefully about the realities I have tried to convey. I want to leave you with a letter that I wrote to a gentleman who was being persuaded to take his company public, and who had asked me to compare that alternative to private equity.

Tatum LLC Memorandum

To: Chuck Gottschalk—Managing Partner Pacific Northwest
From: Doug Tatum
Subject: Thoughts on the Cost of Equity Capital

Chuck, please forward this to the gentleman in Portland who asked if I would take the time to summarize my thoughts on the cost of capital. My point in the presentation was that I felt intuitively that the cost of capital that could be received from a private equity sponsor in today's environment could actually be less than the true cost of capital for equity in a *small* public company.

Using information that I received from a firm that specializes in valuations and has experience with both public and private companies, an estimate for the cost of equity capital for a small public company would range between 18 and 22 percent, depending on the company-specific risk assigned to a particular company. For example 18 percent assumes a 0 percent company-specific risk while 22 percent assumes a 4 percent company-specific risk premium, i.e., the company has earnings volatility in its history, has a short history of earnings, or has customer concentration, etc.

Using the benchmark cost of equity calculation for a small public company, however, does not include the compliance costs that have been estimated by both a quick survey of our partners and an excerpt received from a partner from a Foley and Lardner study to be between $1 million and $3 million. My comment at the speech was that those compliance costs should legitimately be included as an additional cost of capital for a public concern when compared to the cost of capital demanded from a private equity sponsor.

Assuming a $2 million yearly marginal cost of compliance on a $30 million to $40 million public offering would add upward of 5 to 7 percent to the cost of capital.

In summary, this would put the real cost of public capital for a small public company from a low of 23 percent to a high of 29 percent. I believe that the real number is the higher of the two because it would be an unusual company to receive no company-specific risk premium. I believe that a properly negotiated private equity deal would actually cost less and provide a number of other benefits, including:

- More flexibility for additional follow-on rounds of financing
- A more patient point of view on growing the company over the long term
- The ability to actually liquidate founding investors along the way—an IPO is not an exit; in fact, it can lock up founders in some rather difficult ways

I enjoyed catching up with all of our partners at breakfast the next day. Thanks again.

This letter reinforces my point that the decision to bring on outside investors ultimately is about the cost of that capital and the likelihood that it will further the company's progress and increase its value. In many ways, an outside investor can bring to bear a number of appropriate perspectives and pressures that will work for the good of the business, but it will not be easy, and it's not for everyone.

Note: *This is by no means meant to be an exhaustive review of the subject. Getting good legal counsel experienced in securities law and private equity transactions is a requirement when evaluating whether to take on an outside equity investor.*

The BRIDGE Act—an Overview

The BRIDGE Act ("**B**usiness **R**etained **I**ncome **D**uring **G**rowth and **E**xpansion") was introduced in the House on October 9, 2001 (H.R. 3062), by Representatives Jim DeMint (R-SC), Brian Baird (D-WA), Phil Crane (R-IL), Robert Matsui (D-CA), Donald Manzullo (R-IL, Chairman of the House Small Business Committee), Nydia Velazquez (D-NY), Patrick Toomey (R-PA), William Pascrell, Jr. (D-NJ), Ron Lewis (R-KY), and Melissa Hart (R-PA). A companion bill (S. 1903) was introduced in the Senate on January 28, 2002, by Senators John Kerry (D-MA, Chairman, Senate Small Business and Entrepreneurship Committee), Olympia Snowe (R-ME), Joel Lieberman (D-CT), Bob Bennett (R-UT), and Jeff Bingaman (D-NM). In its original form, the BRIDGE Act would have allowed a growing business to *defer* up to $250,000 in federal income tax for two years, with payment over the following four years and with interest paid during the entire deferral period at the federal tax underpayment rate. Businesses that grow at least 10 percent in gross receipts above the prior two-year average would have been eligible if they were on accrual accounting for tax purposes and had $10 million or less in gross receipts. The tax deferral would have expired after 2005 (unless extended), with a General Accounting Office study and report to the Congress.

The BRIDGE Act grew out of extensive discussions with members and staff, business trade groups, and administration officials; two hearings before the House Small Business Committee; as well as the input of my firm, Tatum LLC. Tatum initiated the proposal, based on its experience in providing chief financial officers for emerging growth businesses. Four business trade groups have supported the BRIDGE Act: Council of Growing Companies, National Association of Small Business Investment Companies, Small Business Survival Committee, and Small Business Legislative Council. These groups represent thousands of small and emerging growth businesses and their employees.

The BRIDGE Act would have allowed growing, entrepreneurial businesses to retain a portion of their federal income tax liability for a limited period, payable with interest, during a critical time when outside financing is extremely difficult and costly to obtain. The bill would have provided additional needed capital to be reinvested in the firm's continued growth. This added capital source would have contributed to the creation of up to 641,000 new jobs during the first three years, thus helping to reinvigorate the economy.[52] The Congressional Joint Tax Committee staff estimated that the bill with the 2005 expiration date would have resulted in temporary revenue "losses" during the first four years, followed by revenue pickup during the next six years—for a net revenue *gain* of $1.1 billion for the ten-year period. Thus, there would have been no long-term revenue cost under the bill, since it involved tax deferral, with interest, rather than tax forgiveness.

Had it been enacted, the BRIDGE Act would have helped "bridge" the capital funding gap for entrepreneurial businesses and would have had a significant economic/job/tax revenue multiplier effect, which is still needed in our current economic situation. The bill would have provided critically needed cash for continued business operations. Finally, in getting needed capital to fast-growing, small companies, the BRIDGE Act had the benefit of being highly efficient. George Gendron, editor-in-chief of *Inc.* magazine, stated that "[t]he BRIDGE Act is an ingenious, fiscally sound mechanism for keeping billions in the hands of a group that makes the most efficient use of capital."[53]

Congress once again has a chance to evaluate the BRIDGE Act concept, and I sincerely hope that our country's policy makers will do all that they are able to do to help entrepreneurial growth companies obtain the capital they need to thrive.

Hiring Someone You Can't Afford

The Use of Equity

The Management navigational rule presented in chapter 3 states that a growth company must hire at the top first, not the middle. This requires that a company compete to attract the senior managers and employees that they need in order to navigate successfully through No Man's Land. In chapter 8, I summarized how recent regulatory and accounting changes had profoundly complicated what used to be a very simple and effective way of attracting talent—providing stock options to employees. I developed the example of a French entrepreneurial venture that encountered severe difficulties in its attempt to use equity. In this appendix, let's revisit some issues surrounding the use of equity as a recruiting tool.*

---

*Thanks to Stuart Johnson, a partner with the law firm Powell Goldstein LLP and chair of its Private Equity Practice Team, for his advice and assistance in the review of the materials in this appendix.

Why Use Equity to Recruit?

An emerging growth firm's key advantage when competing for talent is its potential. The best way for a company to share that potential and guarantee a prospective employee's participation is to *give* the employee a share of the equity. I emphasize the word *give* as opposed to *sell*. Remember, the company is recruiting key talent without the ability to pay that talent its true market value on a yearly cash basis. Asking the employee to purchase the equity won't work. A company's only alternative is to create a transaction where a key employee is willing to trade off other employment alternatives for the rights to the potential appreciation of the company's equity. An option, simply put, is the right of that employee to purchase a certain number of shares at a fixed price for a specified time. There are several important benefits of offering stock options to potential employees:

1. The rights to buy shares are usually based on employment, allowing the company to reclaim the units without buying them back if the employee leaves.
2. Stock options set aside shares that can be purchased (exercised) by the employee at a low price if the business is sold at a high price.
3. Historically, options have been structured so that an employee could exercise his or her options in contemplation of a firm's sale and receive tax-favored treatment on the gain.
4. The rights to buy the shares can be based on the time the employee stays with the company or on the achievement of some measurable goal.

How Stock Options Used to Work . . . and How They Work Now

Prior to the new accounting regulations, granting stock options was a very simple exercise that involved a short discussion with an attorney to determine the number of units reserved for the employee, the strike price set for the employee, the period of time over which the grant would be vested, and related issues. Things are different now. Let's go through the table below and analyze what has happened:

United States 2000	United States Now	France 2000
No: Valuation requirements	**Yes:** Valuation requirements	**Yes:** Valuation requirements
No: Special accounting treatment	**Yes:** Special accounting treatment	**Yes:** Special accounting treatment
No: "Qualified options" are not taxable to an individual upon exercise.	**Yes:** "Qualified options" could be taxable to an individual upon exercise.	**No:** "Qualified options" are not taxable to an individual upon exercise.
No: The company is not directly taxed on the employee's gain upon exercise of "nonqualified options."	**No:** The company is not directly taxed on the employee's gain upon exercise of "nonqualified options."	**Yes:** The company is directly taxed on the employee's gain upon exercise of "nonqualified options."

Valuation Requirements and Special Accounting Treatment: Recent changes in the accounting treatment of options requires that a valuation be completed that measures the difference between the strike price (the price at which the employee can buy a share under his or her option agreement) and the value of that share. This measurement determines the income or expense that is recognized in the income statement. For a private company, the valuation process is inexact and further complicates the firm's accounting and auditing requirements. Prior to this new treatment, a company merely footnoted (described in a note to the financial statements) the existence of the options and calculated the "diluted earnings per share" based on a scenario that assumed that the shares under option were ultimately purchased by the employees. The new accounting valuation requirements bring a whole set of new tax complexities to the individuals who receive the grant.

Taxable to the Individual on Issue: Taxability of the options to the employee is a fairly straightforward concept. Traditionally, options were not taxable if granted at what was deemed a fair market value (FMV). Prior to the new accounting requirements, an entrepreneur could for all practical purposes guess the fair market value and establish an appropriate strike price. In just about every case, a reasonable, common-sense approach to establishing a FMV for what is referred to as "qualified stock options" (ISOs) issued pursuant to a qualified Incentive Stock Option plan was defensible. In fact, most companies provided those options at as low a price as they could reasonably justify as FMV to get the employee a head start on building value. Because no real valuation requirements existed in the accounting treatment, many employees got the benefit of a much lower strike price. In many instances, it is an advantage for an entrepreneur in a private company to offer key employees options at a hugely reduced price with the knowledge that the employee would exercise them only upon sale of the company. These options are referred to as nonqualified stock options (NQSOs). The employee loses the tax advantage of the potential capital-gains treatment, but gains the advantage of the cheap stock. The employee exercises at the firm's sale and never has any cash at risk, as he would under a qualified plan that required him to exercise and hold the stock for a year. NQSOs were thus a quite common practice, particularly in a private company hoping to get key employees cheap stock options. Now, however, if the entrepreneur wants to start the employee off with a strike price well below what is deemed FMV based on the company's accounting treatment of the options, the company has to reflect the difference as an expense in the income statement during the year of the grant. Beyond adding all of this accounting complexity to providing options, the real problem for the employee rears its ugly head upon exercise of the options.

Taxable to the Individual on Exercise: U.S. tax law once held that an employee who owned qualified options (ISOs) had to hold them for a given period (two years) and also exercise those options (i.e., purchase the shares) and hold them for one year in order to qualify and receive capital-gains treatment. The bottom line for ISOs was that the employee did not get taxed on the increased value of the shares when the employee exercised his or her options. Remember that as a practical matter for a private company, most options never got exercised until there was reason to think that the company would be sold in the near future. With the valuation requirements imposed on companies today, an employee who might exercise his or her options in advance of the potential sale of a private company must pick up the difference between his or her exercise price and the FMV of the shares. This FMV is reflected in the accounting treatment of the shares for purposes of determining whether AMT tax is due the federal government. The issue of making up the difference did not exist for employees until the new accounting requirements forced a valuation. That gain imposed on the employee is now subject to potential AMT tax. **In other words, because of the valuation requirements of the new accounting treatment on options, an option holder in a private company with no liquidity for the shares that he or she owns might end up paying taxes on the gain.** The double whammy of the accounting treatment and the potential exposure to taxation has all but eliminated the value of options as a tax-advantaged tool to attract senior management into an emerging growth company.

Taxable to the Company upon Exercise: This is not a problem for qualified tax options issued at FMV. However, consider the case of the French firm mentioned in chapter 8. Had the entrepreneur wanted to grant cheap stock options (stock below FMV) to key employees, and had the employees eventually exercised those options at the time the company was sold, the *company* would have faced a social services tax of approximately 45 percent of the gain that the employees received on the stock. This was potentially a huge liability for the company, making the use of cheap stock options prohibitive and kicking off a discussion about whether to move the company to the United States in order to take advantage of the simple manner in which stock options could be provided to a firm's key employees.

What We Are Left with . . .
and Why It's Not as Good

Restricted Stock Grants: Restricted equity grants involve outright issuance of equity to an employee. With a restricted equity arrangement, an employee "vests" in the grant by remaining employed by the company. The firm gets back unvested interests when an employee departs. This is a big problem, since the company now has a former employee with stock. Anyone with stock in a private company enjoys significant rights even as a minority owner and can use these rights to wreak havoc for the company. Another big problem is that the employee gets taxed on the value of the units when the units are no longer restricted. Think about it: An employee gets a huge tax bill for an asset at a point in time and has no cash to pay the tax. After the tax is paid, the stock value can go down and there is no tax loss that the individual can recognize unless he or she sells the units. Good luck selling the stock of a closely held company decreasing in value. And guess what? If the individual has held the stock for a year, he or she can deduct only three thousand dollars of the loss per year unless they have other gains against which to net them.

Phantom Stock: Another possible solution is to just write a contract that creates fake stock or fake options. That way, we avert this mess and get back to what we needed anyway. Phantom stock might work, except for one big problem. When the company is sold and a payment is made to the employee, it is treated as employment income, just like wages. It's a bonus that doesn't qualify for capital-gains treatment, and part of that bonus might be subject to a company's requirement to match employment taxes. In fact, it will be taxed at the employee's highest marginal tax rate, which makes a huge difference. I also suspect that if these vehicles become widely used, the accounting profession will ultimately be required to deal with the substance-over-form issue of their dilution to the common shareholders. But this puts us right back to where we were: reflecting the impact of these vehicles on the firm's income statement in order to remain consistent with the accounting theory that led to the initial valuation requirements.

Conclusion

From an accounting and regulatory standpoint, we have effectively removed most if not all of the simplicity and tax advantages of the techniques that for years have helped entrepreneurial growth companies attract and reward key employees and management. We are now almost at par with the tax policy in France—a slippery slope indeed.

Note: *This overview is by no means meant to be a technical treatise on this subject. Everyone should consult their own tax adviser on how to create equity incentives for their key employees.*

Further Discussion of the Capital Gap

The challenges of the capital gap can seem almost insurmountable given the need to keep fueling your growing company. To meet these challenges, the first and most important step is to forge realistic expectations about what you can expect from the capital markets during this awkward, in-between stage.

Private Equity

Private equity, for all practical purposes, breaks down into several distinct categories. At the risk of oversimplifying, these categories are defined as follows:

Professional Venture Capital Firms: These are funds that specialize in first- and second-round investment for early-stage ideas and companies. Venture capital firms are typically interested in high-tech or certain life sciences or pharmaceutical drug development start-ups. Most venture capital in the United States is concentrated in certain parts of the country. Given the need to monitor their investments, and the time requirements of such monitoring, most VCs don't travel very far.[54] Unless you are building a technology or biotech company and you are located in cities like Boston or San Francisco, it will be tough to get true VC investment for your company.

Corporate Venture Divisions: Many corporations have divisions assigned to look for complementary businesses to invest in. They typically follow the professional venture capital fund model when making investments but will often trade off potential profit from their stock investment in return for trade-offs that benefit their business in other ways, such as guarantees of distribution or license rights in defined fields. Most restrict their activity to investments in technologies or business improvements that fit with their existing business.

Corporate Product Development Divisions: Product development and limited-field licensing can often generate investment in equity by corporations looking to supplement their research and development efforts. This is particularly true in the life sciences but applies to other industries as well. If the product is something they are interested in, a development agreement with meaningful milestone payments can help fund the development and provide working capital. Frequently, such arrangements can be coupled with an equity investment as well.

Angel Investors: These are typically men and women like you, entrepreneurs who have sold their companies and possess readily available capital. Because of who they are, angel investors have an affinity for investing in entrepreneurial growth companies. Many of the major cities have angel investor clubs that can be a source of smaller equity investments. In most cases, you will need follow-up equity investment, coordination of which can be difficult (these groups do not have a fund to draw on, but rely on the interest of the original group for additional investment).[55] The track record for most angel investor groups has been less than encouraging for this class of investment. Angel investors generally do not have the level of professional due diligence and investment monitoring that professional private equity investors employ. However, angel investors can often be a meaningful source of funds.

Uncle Sam: It always makes sense to consider whether a company project can be partly funded by the government under programs designed to foster innovation, such as the Small Business Innovation Research Grant and similar programs. Typically these programs reserve a portion of available research money to private business for product research and development.

Friends and Family: Personal relations are one of the most frequently used capital sources. Again, the amount of capital is usually quite limited. It is important to include your legal counsel in any deal that involves what the securities world regards as "nonqualified investors." It's also important to understand that if you clutter up your capital structure with too many friends and family members as investors, you will end up scaring away the professional investors when you grow large enough to attract them. Professional investors are not interested in private firms with lots of individual minority investors.

Growth or LBO Capital: It is unlikely that you will receive interest from private equity investors in this category until your company can command a $10 million to $15 million valuation based on the company's growth rates and its adjusted cash flow. The markets really open up as soon as your company achieves adjusted cash flows of approximately $10 million and then again when you get to $20 million. These investors are looking for companies that have navigated through No Man's Land and need capital to go into turbo drive. They are also looking for firms that are willing to be bought and that can sustain debt leverage as part of the transaction—hence the name Leverage Buyout (LBO) firms.

Debt

There is a whole category of debt investors, from asset-based lenders to subdebt investors, which I will not describe in detail because they focus even more on cash flow and earnings than friends-and-family early-stage equity investors.

Banks: As I indicated in chapter 5, it is difficult for banks to step up and lend you the money that you will need once the company needs more money than you can afford to repay personally.[56] One of the key issues is for you to concentrate on building a relationship with the bank based on the risk of your business and not on its potential. I have seen many entrepreneurs get a lot out of a banking relationship by establishing a personal relationship with a banker as high up the food chain as possible and by making sure that they do not make the following gaffes:

- Miscommunication: As entrepreneurs, you solve a million problems a day before anyone even knows there is a problem. With banks, you earn credibility when you immediately bring problems to the attention of your sponsor within the bank. You actually reduce the loan's perceived risk in the eyes of your advocate by ensuring that they know what you are dealing with before they end up finding out on their own. They can deal with problems, but they can't stand surprises.
- Misfinancing of assets: It is tempting to use a line of credit that the bank has provided you to buy equipment or anything else you need; this keeps you from going back and asking for more. Yet you really do need to match up the financing with the asset. Don't buy computers with a line of credit that has been provided to fund your receivables and inventory. If the bank won't provide the needed capital for your asset purchase, turn to the vendors you are buying the items from to finance them. There

is a tendency to pass on lease financing offered with the assets that you purchase because of the price of that debt. When transitioning through the capital gap, the *availability* of capital is just as important as its cost. Once assets are purchased, opportunities to obtain lease financing on those assets dry up.

- Misunderstanding negotiation priorities: I have seen too many instances in which the entrepreneur's complete focus in his or her negotiations with the bank is on the interest rate or the price of the debt rather than on its terms. Terms—i.e., the covenants governing the loan—represent the elbow room a firm needs to grow and keep access to the credit. They should be your focus during this transition. Don't congratulate yourself for receiving a prime-rate line of credit if you will be out of covenant with the rate within the second quarter after having received the loan.

Customers and Vendors

This is the area with the most potential for creative solutions. Key customers and vendors have more than a vested interest in your success. I have seen any number of solutions offered up by both customers and vendors that have served to generate desperately needed capital, which in turn have helped propel the company through the capital gap. The real issue here is to approach customers and vendors not on an ad hoc, emergency basis, but rather to treat them as you would any capital provider. Be sure to keep them in the loop and let them know where the risk is in the deal. I can still remember an executive with Data General who would throw his body on the track for the software company that I worked with to buy us the equipment and offer us the terms we needed to keep us afloat while we were growing. I can assure you that we also took some equipment and put it on sale to move it when he needed to make a certain quarter's number. We learned to get and incentivize the salespeople to obtain advances on orders. Although insignificant to most individual customers, the Data General executive's help added up to a nice piece of capital for my company when it needed it most. What can you do in your operations to change the timing of your cash-flow cycle to help create liquidity through the capital gap? When have you last spent some time thinking about your customers and your vendors as capital sources? What kind of deal could you put together to squeeze more cash flow out of the business so as to keep fuel in the tank? Believe me, time spent in this area will be more productive than shopping for equity capital when you are traversing the capital gap.

Conclusion

Unless you believe that you can be attractive to venture capital, you need to concentrate on building revenue, transitioning through No Man's Land, and getting as much capital as you can out of the debt side of your balance sheet. Don't blow your bandwidth trying to find equity investors. Finally and most important, you have to ascertain your company's capital needs in advance of those needs. Doing the creative thinking and tackling the communication issues so as to keep capital in your business cannot be done on an ongoing emergency basis. You have to master the relationship between your business's gas pedal and its fuel gauge. You need, in other words, to know your firm's natural speed limit.

Notes

1. Rich Karlgaard, "Why We Need Startups," *Forbes* (July 21, 2003), 33.

2. Daniel McGinn, "Why Size Matters," *Inc.* (special issue: "America's Fastest Growing Companies," fall 2004), 33.

3. David G. Thomson, *Blueprint to a Billion: 7 Essentials to Achieve Exponential Growth* (Hoboken, NJ: Wiley, 2006), 3.

4. Bo Burlingham, *Small Giants: Companies That Choose to Be Great Instead of Big* (New York: Portfolio/Penguin, 2005), 41.

5. National Commission on Entrepreneurship, *High-Growth Companies: Mapping America's Entrepreneurial Landscape*, 2001.

6. John Case, "The Job Factory," *Inc.* (May 2001).

7. National Commission on Entrepreneurship, *American Formula for Growth: Federal Policy & the Entrepreneurial Economy, 1958–1998*, October 2002.

8. George Hayes and Charles Ou, *A Profile of Owners and Investors of Privately Held Businesses in the United States, 1989–1998*, presented for comment at the Annual Conference of the Academy of Entrepreneurial and Financial Research, 2002.

9. The best resource on alternatives to growth is Bo Burlingham's book *Small Giants*, cited above.

10. First Standard Freight, Inc., is an actual company whose identity has been disguised. Certain information has been altered to maintain the firm's anonymity.

11. "Goldman Sachs: On Top of the World," *The Economist* (April 29, 2006).

12. For a discussion of factors that allow firms to grow to a billion and beyond, see Thomson, *Blueprint to a Billion*.

13. Thomson, *Blueprint to a Billion*, chapter four.

14. Peter F. Drucker, *Management: Tasks, Responsibilities, Practices* (New York: Harper and Row, 1993), 115–19.

15. For further articulation of this point, please see my article, excerpted in Appendix I, "Innovating the Development of Innovation: Gazelles and Corporate R&D," *Research-Technology Management* (May 2007).

16. Quoted in Burlingham, *Small Giants*, 118.

17. Penelope Green, "Saying Yes to Mess," *New York Times* (December 21, 2006), 1.

18. David G. Thomson makes a similar point in his book *Blueprint to a Billion*: "One of the pivotal essentials that enables the other essentials to be simultaneously executed is a strategic leadership pairing in which one leader (or team) faces outward toward markets, customers, alliances, and the community with the other leader (or team) focusing inward so as to optimize operations." Thomson, *Blueprint to a Billion*, 17.

19. Lee W. Mercer, president, National Association of Small Business Investment Companies (NASBIC), statement before the Subcommittees on Tax, Finance, and Exports & Workforce, Empowerment, and Government Programs of the U.S. House of Representatives Committee on Small Business, June 26, 2001.

20. Bo Burlingham makes a similar point using the example of a wine-producing business. See Burlingham, *Small Giants*, 31.

21. E. Floyd Kvamme, cochairman, President's Council of Advisors for Science and Technology, "Beyond the Tax Cut: Unleashing the Economy," hearing before the Subcommittee on Domestic Monetary Policy, Technology, and Economic Growth, House Committee on Financial Services, March 29, 2001.

22. U.S. Small Business Administration, "Small Business Lending in the United States: A Directory of Small Business Lending by Commercial Banks," June 2001, 6.

23. William Morris, ed., *The American Heritage Dictionary of the English Language* (Boston: Houghton Mifflin, 1980).

24. I had been invited by a client and close friend to participate in a meeting with AIG. The meeting was arranged because the client, an international food-trading business, was a major customer of AIG's, purchasing a significant amount of its international credit insurance product. The client had innovated the command and control structure of the food-trading business, and had spun off its technology into a separate company so as to take on the venture capital necessary to get the idea off the ground. It was a good, solid VC deal. This was back in early 2000 when many large corporations sought to start their own venture capital operations and invest directly in early-stage ideas. Our client had been invited to present his firm's idea to an executive who had been placed in charge of AIG's new corporate venture capital.

I was fascinated that in a far-flung, multibillion-dollar operation, the personalized accountability to Mr. Greenburg was so intense that this executive felt uncomfortable with the idea of getting into this business.

"You really don't intend on being in the VC business, do you?" I asked him.

"You're right," he responded.

I don't know the rest of the story, but if the executive kept AIG out of the corporate VC business, he probably saved it a boatload of money. Today AIG is one of the world's largest investors in private equity, which I would guess includes VC funds. Starting their own VC fund and not investing in a fund managed by professional

VCs was a whole different ball game for AIG, and it turned out to be an unmitigated disaster for most companies that tried it. My comments, by the way, aren't intended as a criticism of AIG. Just the opposite: This company is a fascinating example of how even a large company institutionalizes its decision-making process and acts on it in untold ways.

25. Burlingham, *Small Giants*, 112.

26. Lincoln Logistics is an actual company whose identity has been disguised. Certain information has been altered to maintain the firm's anonymity.

27. For a more complete analysis of how the liquidation preferences worked in the Prater deal, please refer to Appendix III.

28. Quoted in "Gov. Easley Announces Sysco to Build Distribution Center in Selma," *US Fed News* (January 26, 2005).

29. Quoted in Peggy Lim, "Sysco, a Beacon for Selma," *News and Observer* (December 16, 2005), D1.

30. Dr. Birch has published a book entitled *Job Creation in America* and has authored numerous articles analyzing the dynamics of business formation and employment growth in America. He received the inaugural NUTEK Prize in 1996 for Entrepreneurship and Small Business Research from the Swedish government. Dr. Birch has pioneered the development of microeconomic analysis techniques. A frequent speaker to national audiences, he is the senior author of the *Corporate Demographics* series, reports that provide information about America's corporate population. Dr. Birch has worked closely with leading financial, manufacturing, and service companies through his former consulting firm, Cognetics Marketing Services.

31. Data in this paragraph is drawn from David Birch, Anne Haggerty, and William Parsons, *Corporate Demographics: Corporate Almanac* (Cambridge, MA: Cognetics, 2000).

32. Conversation with Dr. David Birch, January 3, 2007.

33. National Commission on Entrepreneurship, *American Formula for Growth: Federal Policy & the Entrepreneurial Economy 1958–1998*, October 2002.

34. Edmund S. Phelps, "Dynamic Capitalism," *Wall Street Journal* (October 10, 2006): A14.

35. "Searching for the Invisible Man: Economics Rediscovers the Entrepreneur," *The Economist* (March 11, 2006), 68.

36. Hayes and Ou, *A Profile of Owners and Investors*.

37. Marshall Goldsmith, foreword to Thomson, *Blueprint to a Billion*, x.

38. National Commission on Entrepreneurship, *American Formula for Growth: Federal Policy & the Entrepreneurial Economy, 1958–1998*, October 2002.

39. Interview with Dr. David Birch, New York City, November 7, 2006.

40. Sherwood Ross, "'Gazelles' Providing the Lead in the Nation's Job Creation," *Boston Globe* (May 31, 1994).

41. Interview with Dr. William Baumol, New York City, November 7, 2006.

42. Simtek's story is a remarkable tale in itself. The original entrepreneur had long wanted Harold to take over. When he finally did, following an extraordinary train of circumstances, the results were impressive. Simtek is public (symbol: SMTK) and a client of our firm, so relating the company's transition under Harold's and his team's leadership in any further detail would be self-serving.

43. Interview with Dr. William Baumol, New York City, November 7, 2006.

44. Carl J. Schramm, "Entrepreneurial Capitalism and the End of Bureaucracy: Reforming the Mutual Dialog of Risk Aversion," paper presented at the American Economic Association, Boston, January 6, 2006.

45. Interview with Dr. David Birch, New York City, November 7, 2006.

46. Interview with Dr. William Baumol, New York City, November 7, 2006.

47. Lead sponsors were former South Carolina Congressman (now Republican Senator) Jim DeMint and Democratic Senator and presidential candidate John Kerry. Cosponsors included Republican Senator Olympia Snow and Democratic Congressman Brian Baird. A summary of the bill is included in Appendix IV.

48. Kate O'Beirne, "A Bright Idea on Taxes: How the BRIDGE Act Can Help Small Businessmen and America," *National Review* (March 24, 2003).

49. George Gendron, "Bridging the Capital Gap," *Inc.* (December 2001).

50. "The Home Depot's Bernie Marcus on Why He Couldn't Do It Today," *Investor's Business Daily* (January 30, 2006).

51. Chris Flood, "Family Companies Top Value League," *Financial Times* (January 30, 2007).

52. Projections are based on a sample database from the Kauffman Center for Entrepreneurial Leadership, Kansas City, MO.

53. George Gendron, "Bridging the Capital Gap," *Inc.* (December 2001).

54. Please refer to the Venture Capital Association for details on the size, scope, and location of the VC investments in this country.

55. For an innovative group that has solved this problem for a group of angel investors, check out the Seraph Group. In the interest of full disclosure, I am an investor in Seraph.

56. One resource worth exploring is local SBIC lenders, who typically are interested in smaller loans that are qualified based on size. Their participation helps bridge the capital gap.

Index